EXORCISING YOUR EXCUSES

Heal Your Mind. Honor Your Body.
Manifest Your Dream.

GRIFF NEILSON

authorHOUSE®

AuthorHouse™
1663 Liberty Drive
Bloomington, IN 47403
www.authorhouse.com
Phone: 1 (800) 839-8640

Published by AuthorHouse   02/18/2017

ISBN: 978-1-5246-6030-7 (sc)
ISBN: 978-1-5246-6031-4 (hc)
ISBN: 978-1-5246-6029-1 (e)

Library of Congress Control Number: 2017900792

Print information available on the last page.

CONTENTS

ABOUT THE BOOK

Have you ever sensed that you were meant to experience more from life? Have you ever felt as though you were destined to achieve more? Do you struggle with setting and reaching goals? Are you guilty of denying your desires and dreams because you think they are "unrealistic?" Do you often make excuses that rob you of your true potential?

If you answered "yes" to any of these questions, you likely feel helpless to make positive changes in your life. If you feel stagnant, complacent, or frustrated with the direction of your life, please take heart! In this book, you will be guided through a step-by-step, 60-day plan based on the principles of holistic health that will guarantee you a complete mental overhaul. We will address your mind, your body, your nutrition, and your spirituality. We will teach you essential principles that will help nourish and unify your body, mind, and spirit.

Here is to your new life! I personally challenge you to take the 60-Day Exorcising Your Excuses Challenge and, thereby, live a life of passion, enthusiasm, and excitement! Your journey begins now!

ORIENTATION

Welcome to your journey! I congratulate you for making the commitment to revolutionize your life by exorcising your excuses. Before you begin reading this book, you might be relieved to know that I have laid out action assignments for you in a sixty-day, easy-to-follow format so you can enjoy your journey and not feel overwhelmed during this life-changing process.

This book can be a little intense because it requires a lot of personal change, and I know from experience how demanding change can be. I've written this introduction to give you a personal map that will help you exorcize your excuses. I'm excited for you to begin your journey!

Implementing Your Excuse Exorcisms: Instructions for Action Assignments

The following action assignments are in order by chapters. I recommend that you read the chapter and then implement the corresponding action assignment described below. Some practices, such as water and nutrition, are included from day 1. I've opted to include nutrition and exercise before their respective chapters because they serve as a powerful duo in helping you to promote a healthy mental and physical environment that's conducive to change. I list these every day to help you create new habits through the reprogramming of your subconscious mind. The more you see something, the more you'll reprogram your subconscious mind for the better.

Also note below a daily implementation practice. This will help you to keep yourself accountable and to pace yourself in implementing the concepts taught throughout this book. If you find the suggested implementation schedule too demanding, feel free to add a day where needed. For example, if I give you a two-day time frame to implement the material in a given chapter but you need three, by all means take it.

The key is to stick to the schedule as much as possible so you can integrate and experience the concepts and principles taught in the book. Be honest with yourself, and complete the schedule as close to the sixty-day plan as possible. By doing so, you'll keep your momentum and your motivation. I suggest that you take no more than seventy days to complete the book and implementation schedule as listed below.

I highly recommend the following tips as you begin your personal journey:

- ✓ Set aside at least a half hour per day to work on your daily action assignment. You may find that certain assignments require more time, but you'll need at least thirty minutes.

- ✓ Be sure that you make this a *priority*. Clear your schedule and any possible distractions. Don't make excuses here. If you're hoping to change your life, you must commit to the program 100 percent. Schedule other events around it, *not* the other way around. I know this may sound harsh, but I can assure you that you must make this process a priority to reap the rewards you desire.

- ✓ Many of the action assignments require a place of solitude that allows you to listen to your soul without the interruption of family, friends, or work.

- ✓ Make it very clear to your family and friends that you're committed to the process of exorcising your excuses. Ask them for their help and support. Your journey will be much more enjoyable and rewarding if you have your family and friends on board. Think of them as a dream team ready and willing to help you.

✓ Don't get overwhelmed when you look at your action assignments for the day. You may see up to five items listed, but keep in mind that three of them are likely those that have been listed from day 1, such as exercise, water, and veggie intake. I've tried to keep the action assignments very doable and reasonable. Be sure to read the corresponding chapter *first* because it will give you a clear understanding of the action assignment.

✓ Your six excuse exorcisms officially start from chapter 10 onward. All the action assignments up to that point serve as the foundation for these life-changing powerhouses.

✓ Keep in mind that each of the excuse exorcisms is a lifestyle trait that requires significant practice. In time, you'll reach a level of mastery that will serve you for the rest of your life.

✓ Although I've given you a time frame to complete each excuse exorcism, I don't expect you to master each in that time frame. Rather, practice each one until you feel you've mastered it. Some of them may take up to six months, so be patient, and enjoy the journey.

✓ Stay committed to the practice until it becomes second nature to you. Only through *the mastery* of the excuse exorcisms can you permanently rid yourself of your excuses.

I have formatted the integration schedule in a sequential manner so that each chapter builds on the next. This book isn't meant to be read as buffet-style. Don't pick and choose a chapter that piques your interest. If you read the book in a nonlinear fashion, you'll quickly become confused and overwhelmed. When you read it from cover to cover, it will naturally align with the following action assignments.

Your Official Action Assignment Integration Schedule

Chapter 1

Day 1

- ✓ Read chapter 1.

- ✓ Drink enough water to equal half of your body weight in ounces. For example, if you weight two hundred pounds, you would drink one hundred ounces of clean, pure water. Sports drinks, coffee, and tea don't count here. Water is extremely important for nourishing your brain and allowing an environment that's conducive to learning and reprogramming. Continue this through the remainder of the book—and for the rest of your life.

Day 2

- ✓ Consume at least three vegetables, and keep them as raw as possible. You can lightly steam one out of the three veggies, but don't use heavy cooking techniques, such as pressure cooking or boiling, as these leach your veggies of their nutrients. Consume two to three servings of raw fruit as well. Remember that you're expected to do this every day of this program—and preferably beyond.

- ✓ Reread chapter 1 if necessary.

- ✓ Water intake as described in day 1.

Chapter 2

Day 3

- ✓ Read chapter 2.

- ✓ Water intake as described in day 1.

- ✓ Veggies/fruit as described in day 2.

Day 4

- ✓ Identify the time wasters in your daily schedule, and clear them out. We always find time for our priorities. The lifestyle changes called for in this book may require that you spend less time on activities considered time wasters. Excess TV watching, Internet surfing, texting, social media, and phone calls are probably a good place to start. Be honest with yourself, and see if you can carve out at least a half hour per day (more is better) for personal development.

- ✓ Water intake as described in day 1.

- ✓ Veggies/fruit as described in day 2.

Days 5 to 7

- ✓ Carry a notebook with you, and write down your predominant excuses, as described in chapters 1 and 2. Be sure that you acquaint yourself with the definition of an excuse in chapter 1 so that you know what you're looking for. Be honest with yourself, and remember to look for patterns. For example, if you frequently find yourself using the excuse "I don't have enough time," write it down. Remember you are now becoming *aware* of your predominant excuses so that you can use the steps in the remainder of the book to exorcise your excuses.

- ✓ Water intake as described in day 1.

- ✓ Veggies/fruit as described in day 2.

Chapter 3

Day 8

- ✓ Read chapter 3.

- ✓ Water intake as described in day 1.

- ✓ Veggies/fruit as described in day 2.

Day 9

- ✓ Review the Negative Perception Reality Model in chapter 3. You'll need to be thoroughly acquainted with it to understand the action assignments of the next few days. Consider putting a copy of the model in your home and at work so you can memorize it.

- ✓ Your focus here is stage 1 of the Negative Perception Reality Model. Find a place where you can remain in solitude and reflect on your childhood and early adulthood. Recall that when you want something, such as food or a toy, you take whatever action is necessary to get it.

- ✓ If possible, observe young children, and notice how their desires equal action. They are unencumbered by conditioned beliefs. They don't host internal dialogues of what they can't do, and they certainly don't entertain their limitations. Rather, they simply take action toward their desired outcome, and if they can't get it, they often cry or show extreme displeasure.

- ✓ Take mental notes of the barriers that you place on your goals and desires. How many times do you talk yourself out of the desires of your heart based on your internal programming?

- ✓ Water intake as described in day 1.

- ✓ Veggies/fruit as described in day 2.

Day 10

✓ Your focus here is stage 2 of the Negative Perception Reality Model. Find a place in which you will be undisturbed and identify your own forms of personal conditioning. This is a great way to peer inside of your head and identify some of your condition beliefs.

✓ In particular, write down how you have been *conditioned* to think in the following areas:

  o parental conditioning (What was the overlying theme of your parents' teachings? Identify what you belief to be positive, neutral, and negative forms of conditioning that still influences you today.)
  o family
  o political (Where are you one the political spectrum and why?)
  o religious (What do you believe and why?)
  o educational (What do you believe about education and your own responsibilities regarding it?)
  o social conditioning/expectations (What do you feel is expected of you by society and by peers?)
  o athletics/sports/exercise
  o nutrition (What is good and what is bad?)
  o importance of being popular as a kid
  o importance of keeping up with the Joneses as an adult
  o your genetic predispositions and limitations (What are you blessed with or limited by as a result of your genes?)
  o mental ability/inability

✓ Feel free to identify any form of conditioned belief not listed. Keep in mind that you don't have to elaborate on these conditioned beliefs at this point. For now, just identify them.

✓ Water intake as described in day 1.

✓ Veggies/fruit as described in day 2.

Days 11 and 12

    ✓ Your focus here is stages 3 through 5 in the Negative Perception Reality Model.

    ✓ Stage 3: Using the conditioned beliefs that you listed from stage 2 (day 10), identify which beliefs are self-limiting to your personal development. These are the beliefs that keep you from living the life of your dreams. A good example of this would be the belief that you're too busy to eat well because you lack the ability to prepare your food in advance.

    ✓ Stage 4: Identify how your limiting beliefs have translated into action. If you use the excuse of being too busy, you'll likely take action on that belief by doing nothing to change your behavior. The action then is inaction. If you believe you're too busy to prepare healthy food, you'll naturally find that you do *nothing* for food preparation. Instead, you continue to take action on your belief through the consumption of fast or processed foods.

       Other examples include the belief that you are not smart or athletic, so you take action by *not* taking tough college courses or trying out for a sports team. Your key is to find the limiting beliefs that have led you to actions (or inactions) and that continue to take you away from your dreams and desires. Remember—inaction is still action because it's a decision and a choice.

    ✓ Stage 5: Look at your life holistically (physically, mentally, emotionally, and spiritually), and describe in detail how your limiting beliefs have contributed to your current circumstances. Using our previous example of being too busy, you could describe how you've avoided exercise, healthy food preparation, and other life-affirming activities because of your conditioned belief. You could further describe how the belief has added to weight gain, health problems, and self-esteem issues. In short, become aware of the cause-and-effect nature of your conditioned beliefs. If done properly, this exercise can be life changing because it will show you the consequences of your conditioned beliefs and excuses.

- ✓ Water intake as described in day 1.

- ✓ Veggies/fruit as described in day 2.

Chapter 4

Days 13 and 14

- ✓ Read chapter 4.

- ✓ Add twenty minutes of exercise into your daily routine if you haven't already done so. You should increase your time by five minutes every other week until you reach one hour. Start light if you're unaccustomed to exercise, and build up from there. Simply walking is a good place to start if you have been sedentary for six months or more. If you feel intimidated by exercise, hire a qualified personal trainer who can help you through the process.

- ✓ Water intake as described in day 1.

- ✓ Veggies/fruit as described in day 2.

Days 15 and 16

- ✓ Stages 3 through 5 of the Positive Perception Reality Model found in chapter 4 is our focus here.

- ✓ Stage 3: Here we're going to look at the desires of your heart versus your "mind stories." Using our example from the last chapter, let's say that you would like to get six-pack abs but you house the limiting belief that you're too busy. In this case, you would write something similar to the following:

o   Desire of my heart: "Get in shape and have a six-pack I'm proud of."

o   Mind story: "I don't have enough time to work out that hard and be that strict in my diet. I need to be reasonable, so I'll wait until life slows down a little and start then."

✓   Write down *all* the desires of your heart that you've silenced over the years. This can be a fun and liberating exercise—if you take time to listen to the desires of your heart.

✓   Your next step is to form beliefs that are *opposite* of your limiting beliefs. Using the example above, you would state,

o   "I make time for health and fitness, and I enjoy it."

o   "I also enjoy having a six-pack and feeling healthy and in shape."

Note: This exercise takes courage because your subconscious mind will likely throw a fit when you consciously entertain ideas that you have previously deemed impossible or unrealistic. You'll likely feel very uncomfortable when you go head-to-head with the current programming of your subconscious mind, so be sure to hang in there. Remember—you are now in reprogramming mode, so enjoy the journey. Use the examples in chapter 4 to stoke your mind and give you places to search in your own life.

✓   Be sure to isolate *all* your mind stories and then form beliefs opposite to all of them. This process can take months. It will be ongoing for the rest of your life as you create new mind stories.

✓   Repeat these beliefs audibly and with emotion at least two times per day, preferably in the morning after arising and before bedtime. I would recommend affirming them as often as you possibly can.

✓   Water intake as described in day 1.

✓   Veggies/fruit as described in day 2.

✓   At least twenty minutes of exercise.

Chapter 5

Day 17

- ✓ Read chapter 5.

- ✓ Water intake as described in day 1.

- ✓ Veggies/fruit as described in day 2.

- ✓ At least twenty minutes of exercise.

Days 18 and 19

- ✓ Recognize that the desires of your heart come from your Highest Self, as described throughout this book. For example, if you have the desire "I want to start my own business," recognize that it comes from your Highest Self and that you may have blocked it out with so-called reasoning or an excuse. Your desires should be honored as part of your Highest Self, and, as such, they need to be explored and lived. Take the time to entertain the desires of your heart and to reflect on them. The next step is to *act* on them.

- ✓ Begin to monitor your internal dialogue for excuse making or conditioned beliefs that lead to excuse making.

- ✓ When you eliminate excuse making and negative internal dialogues from your thinking patterns, begin at once to employ the triple-A solution, described in chapter 5.

- ✓ Water intake as described in day 1.

- ✓ Veggies/fruit as described in day 2.

- ✓ At least twenty minutes of exercise.

Chapter 6

Day 20

- ✓ Read chapter 6.

- ✓ Water intake as described in day 1.

- ✓ Veggies/fruit as described in day 2.

- ✓ At least twenty minutes of exercise.

Days 21 and 22

- ✓ Identify the predominant "themes and memes" in your life. How are they contributing to your excuse-making patterns? For example, if you suffer from the meme that states, "I'm overweight because I'm genetically predisposed," how might it be encouraging the excuses that you use to justify your poor nutritional habits? In this example, the themes and memes are driving a belief that subsequently drives an excuse (for example, "I am genetically predisposed to be overweight, so why should I even try to exercise?").

- ✓ Identify the times in your life when you formed personal themes and memes. Where did they come from (parents, school, friends, etc.), and when did you start to believe them to be your personal truth?

- ✓ Remember that your themes and memes lead directly to conditioned beliefs and excuse-making patterns. *Only after you identify your themes and memes will you be able to understand where your excuse making is coming from.*

- ✓ A few themes and memes to look for:

  o   personal values
  o   health and fitness

- o nutrition
- o finances
- o religion
- o relationships
- o friends (what a true friend should be and what a friend is)
- o your personal abilities or lack thereof (what you're good at and what you're bad at)

Chapter 7

Day 23

- ✓ Read chapter 7.

- ✓ Water intake as described in day 1.

- ✓ Veggies/fruit as described in day 2.

- ✓ At least twenty minutes of exercise.

Day 24

- ✓ Buy Dr. Bruce Lipton's 2005 book, *The Biology of Belief,* and read it after you finished this assignment. It will give you profound insights into the nature-versus-nurture debate.

- ✓ Consider the important truth that you have the ultimate say in your life. Your health and vitality are the sum of what you eat, drink, think, and exercise.

- ✓ Water intake as described in day 1.

- ✓ Veggies/fruit as described in day 2.

- ✓ At least twenty minutes of exercise.

Chapter 8

Day 28

- ✓ Read chapter 8.

- ✓ Water intake as described in day 1.

- ✓ Veggies/fruit as described in day 2.

- ✓ At least twenty minutes of exercise.

Days 29 to 35

- ✓ Create a rough draft of your Crystal-Clear Vision (CCV). This is the most important action assignment of the entire book. Use the steps outlined in chapter 8, and don't be fooled into thinking that it needs to be perfect. You have six days to complete this, so take time to go inward and find out what you really want to create in your life.

- ✓ Your CCV will evolve naturally during your life, so update it at least once per year to reflect your current state of being. However, your core values and principles remain steady throughout your life.

- ✓ Water intake as described in day 1.

- ✓ Veggies/fruit as described in day 2.

- ✓ At least twenty minutes of exercise.

Chapter 9

Day 36

- ✓ Read chapter 9.

- ✓ Water intake as described in day 1.

- ✓ Veggies/fruit as described in day 2.

- ✓ At least twenty minutes of exercise.

Days 37 to 39

- ✓ Set your SMART Goals using the guidelines in chapter 9.

- ✓ Water intake as described in day 1.

- ✓ Veggies/fruit as described in day 2.

- ✓ At least twenty minutes of exercise.

Chapter 10: Excuse Exorcism 1

Day 40

- ✓ Read chapter 10.

- ✓ Water intake as described in day 1.

- ✓ Veggies/fruit as described in day 2.

- ✓ At least twenty minutes of exercise.

Day 41

- ✓ Have somebody assess your breathing and note how many natural (unforced) breaths you take per minute. A good optimal range is twelve to sixteen breaths per minute. If you exceed this number, chances are good that your sympathetic nervous system is overly active and therefore creating unnecessary stress on your entire body.

✓ Practice breathing diaphragmatically for five minutes. Breathe in through your nose and into your stomach. Your chest should not rise until the last quarter of your inhalation. If you find this difficult, you likely have a faulty breathing pattern. As your mental and physical fitness levels improve, your breathing naturally improves.

✓ The more you practice breathing correctly, the faster you'll correct your faulty breathing patterns. Be sure that you practice in a *nonstressful* environment. This will ensure a healthy balance between your sympathetic and parasympathetic nervous systems.

✓ Practice this daily until it becomes second nature to you.

✓ Water intake as described in day 1.

✓ Veggies/fruit as described in day 2.

✓ At least twenty minutes of exercise.

Day 42

✓ Use the listed in chapter 10 under the "Posture" subheading to begin working on your posture. Work on this daily until you are subconsciously retrained. Remember your ears should be in line with your shoulder, your shoulder in line with your hips, and your hips in line with your knees and ankles. Simply search Google Images for a good image of correct posture to use as a visual cue.

✓ Get at least thirty minutes of exercise starting *today*. Be sure that you incorporate weight training into your routine at least three times per week. If you're a beginner, consider hiring a good personal trainer or getting a good book to help you incorporate this into your life.

✓ Water intake as described in day 1.

✓ Veggies/fruit as described in day 2.

Days 43 and 44

✓ Here you work on your tone of voice. Use the suggestions made at the end of chapter 10 to supercharge your tone.

✓ This will take some time to correct if you're a certified pessimist. My recommendation is to wear something, such as a ring or a watch with an alarm, to remind you about your tone of voice. This can also remind you about your breathing and posture.

✓ Keep in mind that this should be an ongoing process until you reprogram yourself to speak with a more positive tone. Typically, this process takes anywhere from three weeks to two months, depending on how engrained your negative tones have become.

✓ Get at least thirty minutes of exercise up to six times per week. Be sure that at least three of the six days are devoted to weight training.

✓ Water intake as described in day 1.

✓ Veggies/fruit as described in day 2.

Chapter 11: Excuse Exorcism 2

Day 45

✓ Read chapter 11.

✓ Get at least thirty minutes of exercise up to six times per week. Be sure that at least three of the six days are devoted to weight training.

✓ Water intake as described in day 1.

✓ Veggies/fruit as described in day 2.

Days 46 and 47

- ✓ Here you're becoming aware of predominating internal dialogues that are subconsciously shaping your current behavior.

- ✓ Complete the action steps included at the end of chapter 11.

- ✓ Keep in mind that internal dialogues are the culmination of the mind stories, excuses, and conditioned beliefs that we covered in chapters 4 to 7. To make this process easier, refer to the notes I had you take in these chapters. They will help you become aware of your negative internal dialogues.

- ✓ Get at least thirty minutes of exercise up to six times per week. Be sure that at least three of the six days are devoted to weight training.

- ✓ Water intake as described in day 1.

- ✓ Veggies/fruit as described in day 2.

Chapter 12: Excuse Exorcism 3

Day 48

- ✓ Read chapter 12.

- ✓ Get at least thirty minutes of exercise up to six times per week. Be sure that at least three of the six days are devoted to weight training.

- ✓ Water intake as described in day 1.

- ✓ Veggies/fruit as described in day 2.

Days 49 to 51

✓ Use the "Step-by-Step Guide to Unifying Your Brain," found in chapter 12.

✓ Keep in mind that this process can take much more than three days. Take whatever amount of time you need. You can either pause here for a while or continue to do this daily as you move through the rest of the book. I recommend the latter to keep a good pace.

✓ Get at least thirty minutes of exercise up to six times per week. Be sure that at least three of the six days are devoted to weight training.

✓ Water intake as described in day 1.

✓ Veggies/fruit as described in day 2.

Chapter 13: Excuse Exorcism 4

Day 52

✓ Read chapter 13.

✓ Get at least thirty minutes of daily exercise up to six times per week. Be sure that at least three of the six days are devoted to weight training.

✓ Water intake as described in day 1.

✓ Veggies/fruit as described in day 2.

Days 53 to 55

- ✓ Implement the five nutritional principles listed under "Your Ultimate Solution" in chapter 13.

- ✓ As with the other excuse exorcisms, this practice will take longer than two days to form a new habit. Employ these nutritional principles for a minimum of two months to form a new habit. But your assignment here is to start your journey *today*.

- ✓ Get at least thirty minutes of exercise up to six times per week. Be sure that at least three of the six days are devoted to weight training.

- ✓ Water intake as described in day 1.

- ✓ Veggies/fruit as described in day 2.

Chapter 14: Excuse Exorcism 5

Day 56

- ✓ Read chapter 14.

- ✓ Get at least thirty minutes of exercise up to six times per week. Be sure that at least three of the six days are devoted to weight training.

- ✓ Water intake as described in day 1.

- ✓ Veggies/fruit as described in day 2.

Day 57

- ✓ Select one of the three meditative practices listed in chapter 14, and devote yourself to twenty minutes of daily practice. *This is a practice that you should have for the rest of your life.* If this sounds daunting, just give it three weeks, and you'll never want to turn back. I promise!

✓ Keep in mind that there are countless other methods of slowing your mind, and you are more than welcome to try them as well. The point of meditation is to slow your mind and therefore allow your body, mind, and spirit to rejuvenate so you can thrive holistically.

✓ Get at least thirty minutes of exercise up to six times per week. Be sure that at least three of the six days are devoted to weight training.

✓ Water intake as described in day 1.

✓ Veggies/fruit as described in day 2.

Chapter 15: Excuse Exorcism 6

Day 58

✓ Read chapter 15.

✓ Get at least thirty minutes of exercise up to six days per week. Be sure that at least three of the six days are devoted to weight training.

✓ Water intake as described in day 1.

✓ Veggies/fruit as described in day 2.

Days 59 and 60

✓ This one has already been covered by virtue of you exercising for the last month and a half. Congratulations!

✓ The only new assignment is to employ small bouts of exercise when you find yourself slipping into negative internal dialogues that affect the way you think and feel. For example, if you're having a bad day, and you're beginning to see the glass as half empty, take five or ten minutes out of your day to move your body and exercise. Do it on the spot! The point is to release your natural feel-good hormones and neurotransmitters and to move the fluid and energy in your body. When you do this, you stave off a mental state that is conducive to excuse making.

✓ Water intake as described in day 1.

✓ Veggies/fruit as described in day 2.

INTRODUCTION

Winter was still heavy in the air during March 2007, but signs of new life hinted of spring. As a personal trainer, my hopes were high as I anticipated the arrival of a new client. His name was Doug, and one of my very successful former clients had referred him to me.

As I watched Doug walk up to our front door, I couldn't help recall that my client had warned me that Doug was a "special case" and that I would have to use every tool I had to help him. Little did I know that I was about to learn a profound life lesson that has changed the way I view why some people succeed while others continually struggle.

Doug was a seemingly normal man: average in looks and a little above average in fitness. He sported a typical American beer gut that had not yet run amuck. Doug had been working out for about twenty-five years, and he was frustrated. As most people do, he lost weight and then put it right back on—and then some. He could never get his nutrition under control, and his self-concept and self-image had been chronically and cyclically dragged through the mud.

Doug was friendly and respectful, and he made a decent living. He was single and had never married in his fifty-four years. I thought nothing of his marital status until I began to learn about his mental barriers, which had been nurtured in his mind from the time he was a little boy.

I met with Doug once a week and spent hours talking about his goals, his fears, his ambitions, and—most importantly—his mind-set. I enjoyed my conversations with him, as I found his story interesting and his challenges intriguing. I would often greet Doug with a question: "So how are you treating life?" He would grin and then coarsely state, "Life's a bitch." This bold expression, although uttered with a joking tone, was a window into his soul, which would later spill out in my office.

I was responsible for helping Doug get into the best shape of his life, and we agreed that it was a worthy goal. I did all the things a good personal trainer should do. I wrote him a customized exercise program that I'm still proud of today. I had him track his food intake in a food journal, and I tried to motivate him at every turn. Doug told me that if I were to be graded as a personal trainer, I'd receive an A+.

After six weeks of training, Doug had lost three pounds. But then he turned around in a Jekyll-and-Hyde fashion and put five pounds back on. I was shocked. How could this be? I was doing everything I'd learned about in school and was following my personal training certifications to the letter of the law. I scratched my head, wracked my brain, and stood there in a state of bewilderment after evaluating his regression.

This was a valuable turning point in my career. I began to ask myself deep and probing questions: What are the unforeseen barriers that keep surfacing in Doug's life and cause him to indulge in self-defeating behaviors? How could he come to the gym, get motivated, put a smile on his face, commit that he would "do better," and then arrive the next week with the same worn-out story as to why he had failed in reaching his goals?

I was determined to answer these questions, not only for Doug but also for myself. I began to dig in. I had long conversations with Doug, probing him with questions about his nutrition and asking him why he felt he could not abide by the program. At one time, I asked him why he didn't eat more frequently during the day; he skipped breakfast, ate at ten, and then didn't eat again until six. In response to this question, he told me that his day was too busy and that it took too much time to prepare food to fill in the gaps.

As I continued to have intriguing conversations with Doug, I found myself nodding in agreement with him. He always seemed to have a very good reason why he wasn't following his nutritional program. He would offer me statements like "I don't have time," "I eat junk food for relief when I'm stressed," and "Health food is just too darn expensive." He frequently gave these and similar reasons to defend his less-than-stellar nutrition.

Doug was also replete with reasons for why he couldn't adopt a healthy lifestyle. He would often say, "I'm just a loser and can't keep up with the program" or "I have never had a high degree of self-control" or "My genetics are rigged against me." These reasons are only the top of a towering mountain of those he frequently cited.

When I first conversed with Doug about his reasons, I felt hopeless and confused. I found myself thinking, *Yeah, he has a point there*, or *Sounds like he's a victim of his circumstances; no wonder this poor man has never changed.* I was struggling as a personal trainer because all the reasons he threw out made sense to me. In other words, *most* of the reasons stood up to three things:

1. They were reasonable.
2. They were justifiable.
3. They were supported by his circumstances.

Shortly after this experience, I had the privilege of reading one of the most life-changing books that I've ever read, *Excuses Begone* by Dr. Wayne W. Dyer. As I read the first chapter, I experienced what can only be called an aha moment—a moment of life-changing insight. I finally realized that the so-called reasons that Doug was giving me were not reasons at all. They were nothing more than unadulterated excuses.

With this revelation, I began to examine my own life and find issues that I had excused away. It was a moment of reckoning for me. I suddenly knew that each rational reason Doug had given me was an excuse masquerading as a reason why he could not accomplish the desire of his heart.

This eureka moment forever changed the way I think and the way I see life. I now have the ability to diagnose my own excuse-laden thinking patterns. With this awareness, I'm able to replace my excuse-making tendencies with thinking patterns that *propel* me toward my goals.

Many years have passed since I talked with Doug, and I look back on that experience with fondness because it was a turning point. It was the catalyst for me to study personal development. I began to read every personal development book I could get my hands on, and I began to apply them to my life. A few years later, I went back to school in holistic health and am now certified as level 3 Holistic Lifestyle coach through the CHEK Institute. Through this and other experiences, I've come to understand why we human beings act the way we do.

My research and experience have led to this book. It's the only book of its kind because it offers a comprehensive and holistic approach to eradicating excuses in your life. We will explore and discover hidden areas of your life that are secretly and unconsciously contributing to your personal frustrations, limitations, and failures. We'll also look at excuse making from a novel holistic vantage point that has never been explored formally.

The primary aim of this book is to help you identify and eradicate the self-limiting thoughts and excuses that have sabotaged you in the past. Make no mistake about it: if you have fallen short of any goal in your life, you can *always* trace your result back an excuse. You're about to find out why this happens and how you can proactively change the programming in your mind so *you and only you* become the author of your life—and you live it on your terms.

If you're tired of starting strong and losing momentum every time you seek personal change, this book is for you. You'll learn about what an excuse is and how excuse making can control your destiny if you don't combat it with awareness. You'll learn that you and you alone are in control of your habitual thinking patterns. And you'll learn about the seeming paradox of "losing your mind" to reprogram your mind. I am honored to have you here, and I invite you to open your mind to the concepts that follow, so they will enhance your life as they have mine.

Life is good!

CHAPTER 1

EXCUSES DEFINED

Are You Living a Lie?

He that is good for making excuses is seldom good for anything else.
—Benjamin Franklin

So here you are, not living the life you want to live. As you walk past the mirror, you notice more of yourself than normal. Slightly embarrassed, you mutter, "How did this happen?" As you wonder why you're looking a little more plump than usual, you hear the chatter of your busy mind explaining, "I'm busy," "I don't have time to exercise right now," "Once I am done with my project at work, I can get serious about fitness again," or "I have to take care of others before myself."

These and countless other excuses parade through your mind in a desperate attempt to lessen your embarrassment. However, even after an honorable attempt to justify your figure, you scratch your head in confusion because your excuses have made you feel worse. Why? They didn't change what's staring back at you in the mirror.

Excuses Defined: Do You Pass the Three-Tier Test?

One of the hardest tasks in becoming excuse-free is identifying what qualifies as an excuse and what doesn't. How do you know when you're making an excuse and when you aren't? After all, you don't have time, and your job is demanding right now, right? To help you with this question, let me suggest two definitions of *excuse*:

1. Any rational, justifiable, or reasonable explanation as to why you can't accomplish your desires
2. Any time you forget about your ultimate potential

Let's cover the first one. Most excuses hide under the guise of being rational, justifiable, or reasonable. Take, for example, the biggest excuse in America: lack of time. Not having enough time seems to be an accepted reality for all of us. I know that you're busy, and so are your uncle and your uncle's goldfish. Nobody is immune to it. With these facts in mind, we can describe an excuse as rational, justifiable, and reasonable.

Wow! No wonder these little jewels known as excuses make you feel better about yourself. If you can pass the aforementioned three-tier test, you should be out of the woods, right? You aren't really making an excuse if it's reasonable, justifiable, or rational, right?

Wrong!

The reality is that you still have that nagging voice in the back of your head telling you that you need to change. How irritating! The proverbial mirror never lies. You may ask yourself, "How can this be?" After all, you have a rational, justifiable, or reasonable explanation for not accomplishing your goal, right? So why do you still feel like something is not right within you?

The Test

Here's a simple test you can use to find out if you're indeed making an excuse: if your logical, reasonable, or justifiable reason for not taking action puts a barrier between you and your goal, you know without a doubt that you are making an excuse. (Keep in mind that this test is valid even after you go through the aforementioned three-tier test.)

Say, for example, you want to get in better shape, but you find yourself continually saying that you're too busy and don't have enough time to get to the gym. You back up your statements with your schedule, proving that you really don't have time to exercise. Although your reason is rational, justifiable, or reasonable, it still limits you from reaching your goal. No matter how you try to spin it, this is an excuse because it limits your personal development and divides you from your goal.

Your Nature

The struggle here is that you are a human being. As a human being, you were designed and created to better yourself on a continual basis. This is literally hardwired within your DNA for your survival. Think of a time when you wanted to accomplish something, but you ended up making an excuse instead. When this happened, you placed your very essence into a state of developmental decline. In other words, any time you make an excuse instead of reaching for your goal, you negate your God-given ability to create victories in your life. In essence, you forfeit your ability to develop as a human being and thereby don't meet your potential.

This leads us to the second definition of excuse making. Before I discuss this definition, let me be very clear about my personal beliefs and experience with excuse making. I believe that we are all creations and expressions of God, and as such, we have limitless potential to achieve anything that inspires us. If you have the inkling, hunch, or desire to better yourself in any way, those desires should be respected and viewed as inspiration from the Higher Source.

> If your logical, reasonable, or justifiable reason for not taking action puts a barrier between you and your goal, you know without a doubt that you're making an excuse.

When we *forget* that we have such divine potential, we default to excuse making. In his book *Excuses Begone,* Wayne W. Dyer defines an excuse as a "misalignment." When you make excuses, you forget about your limitless potential, which prevents you from reaching your ultimate potential.

When you make an excuse, you falsely believe that external circumstances are limiting you. Furthermore, you falsely believe that you're a victim of those external circumstances. In his book *Outwitting the Devil,* Napoleon Hill coined a term that he referred to as "the other self." The other self is the side of you that doesn't make excuses and walks in faith toward any goal that you've been inspired to make. When you experience your other self, you don't think of all the reasons you can't accomplish something; rather, you focus on all the reasons you can and will.

> We are all creations and expressions of God, and as such, we
> have limitless potential to achieve anything that inspires us.

When you operate from this other self, you don't think in terms of limitations, difficulties, or impossibilities, which are all forms of fear. In this mind-set, you feel energized, inspired, and unstoppable. I trust that you've had these moments in your life. Recall a time when you felt inspired. You probably felt that you could not and would not be stopped, despite obstacles in your path. In this state, you weren't capable of making excuses. You chose to view all obstacles as blessings in disguise that were designed to teach you and make you stronger.

At this point, if you find your mind coming up with excuses, such as, "Yeah, well, that's nice, and it sounds good, but I live in the real world with real challenges and problems," I respectfully invite you to consider three things:

1. Life will not slow down for you in the near or distant future.
2. It is your responsibility to live excuse-free despite your circumstances.
3. It is your birthright to live in an excuse-free inner world.

Let's discuss these three important truths in turn, starting with the first one. For most people, lack of time is the number-one excuse. However,

I think it's appropriate to realize that life is never going to slow down for you.

Procrastination is one of the most damaging effects of making excuses. If we are indeed too busy, we have no choice but to put our goals on the back burner for a future date. This in and of itself keeps us trapped in a vicious cycle of expecting life to slow down so we can accomplish our goals. In this state of mind, we fail to recognize that our goals and ambitions are slipping further and further away.

> If you have and inkling, hunch, or desire to better
> yourself in any way, that desire should be respected and
> viewed as inspiration from the Higher Source.

Remember—it's merely an illusion that life will slow down. The only way we can make time for exercise and healthy eating habits is to make them priorities. To start your journey of exorcising your excuses, look at your daily schedule and activities and do the following: look for time wasters that you can discard, such as TV watching, Internet surfing, phone calling, excessive texting, and any other activity that can be minimized to an appropriate time frame. Don't fool yourself on this. Most people can delete some useless activities. When you eliminate time wasters, you can fill your time with exercising and preparing healthy food.

Let's look at the second reason you aren't the exception to the rule: it is your responsibility to live excuse-free despite your circumstances. If you truly desire to live excuse-free, you must take this literally. You are not the exception. However large my trials and travails are, they are equaled or trumped by what other people are going through.

Let's be very clear here. Life will get hectic, and it will throw curve balls at you. You will have times of depression, anxiety, and fatigue. You will have times when you feel mentally sluggish and unmotivated. As hard as this seems, it doesn't excuse you from staying true to your desire. The reason for this is simple: *life will always happen.*

If you aren't overly busy at this time, you might be a little down about a relationship. If you aren't experiencing a bout of depression, you might have anxiety about a new job responsibility and that jerk of a boss that never gives you a break. If you have the best boss in the world and your work is fine, you might be consumed with a volunteer project that takes many hours of your day and adds significant stress to your life.

When you resort to excuse making, you forget about your limitless potential, and thus your false beliefs lead to actions that are not conducive to your ultimate potential.

Your goal is to not allow yourself to make an excuse. Here is a promise that will inspire you to action: your life will get easier when you clear out the excuses and make time for your priorities.

Take exercise as an example. Numerous studies indicate that aerobic exercise reduces anxiety, stress, depression, ADHD, and addictions. Wow! When we choose to prioritize things that are good for us, our lives magically become a little bit easier. Human beings have a perpetual problem: we tend to focus on how hard change will be. We rarely focus on the benefits of change. We rarely understand how change can bring pleasure into our lives.

Finally, it is *your birthright to live excuse-free.* Making excuses chips away at your consciousness and at your character. If you excuse away inaction, you incur a guilt that won't leave until you face and correct your excuses.

Excuse making is analogous to loading a pickup truck with bricks. Each excuse you make is a brick loaded into your mind. With each succeeding brick, you add more mental weight. When you load too many bricks, you lose horsepower and become bogged down. This becomes an extremely discouraging and cumbersome mental activity that both limits your divine potential and keeps you stuck in your excuses.

When you live in your excuses, you may be tempted to believe that this state of being is normal. Nothing could be further from the truth. Your natural state of being is excuse-free. When you were a child and wanted something, you didn't let anything stand in your way. If you wanted cookies, you set out to get them peacefully or by force. If you wanted to raise money, you put up a lemonade stand and got it done.

So why did this change? Why do you set a goal and then question yourself and talk yourself out of it? Why do you have to set the same goal one hundred times with an inner knowing that you'll ultimately fail at it? Is this your fate? In the next chapter, I'll delve into why this happens and give you clear instructions on how to change it. I'm excited to help you scrub the excuses out of your brilliant and limitless brain.

CHAPTER 2

HABITOLOGY

Discovering Why You Do the Things You Do

There are certain things that, for want of ability to change, one must embrace.
Because if the same ingrained habits constantly worsen your life,
at least you aren't just repeating yourself.
—Benson Bruno

Humans are creatures of habit. We're on autopilot much of the time as we work, eat, and interact with others. Unfortunately, some of our habits are not so healthy, such as overeating, smoking, overspending, being negative, and so on. While all of us have shadow traits that we would prefer remain private, you can take heart. You are now going to become aware of what's driving your habitual actions and to learn the necessary steps to correct them.

It's time for a confession. In the not-so-distant past, I believed that I was a victim of my external circumstances. I believed that many of my misfortunes were a direct consequence of the actions of others or the result of serendipitous events. In other words, I wasn't willing to take responsibility for how my life was taking shape.

But because life is the ultimate teacher, I've learned that I can't blame other people or external situations for my flaws. Initially this was hard for me to accept. Yes, some external circumstances are uncontrollable, and I don't deny that they can profoundly influence us. However, I'm convinced that we can—and must—control how we react to external circumstance because they have the ability to teach us or to destroy us.

Take, for example, one of my past clients, whom I'll call Linda. One of my most successful clients referred Linda to me. Linda had been told that I could help with any problem she had, so she was expecting the world. Little did I know that I was in for another life-changing experience.

When I met with Linda, I felt energy being sucked out of me. It was as though somebody was siphoning the energy from my soul. After I asked about her goals, she revealed her true colors by stating, "I just have had the worst luck over the years, and I can't seem to get any sustainable momentum." Little did I know that she would utter countless similar statements, such as, "I am so old," "I'm a loser," "I just can't get it together," "people are judging me," "I'm not losing weight fast enough," "I am sick of healthy food," and so on and so on.

Without yet knowing the cause of her continued failures, I opted to bury my head in the sand and disregard all her reasons for not succeeding. Instead of getting to the root of her problem and doing some life coaching, I opted to jump right into the personal training portion of her program.

What followed was predictable. I designed an exercise and nutrition program for her and tried to get her "pumped" to follow it. I felt a false sense of accomplishment as she nodded in agreement. I told myself, *If I can just get her exercising, it should take care of the rest.* How terribly wrong I was!

Linda exercised, but only when she was with me. She never exercised by herself or followed the program as outlined. Initially she began to eat better, but only for two to three days at a time. I began to pull my hair out as I realized that nothing seemed to last with her.

At the beginning of her next session, I pulled her into my office and canceled our workout because I'd had what was akin to a revelation, a proverbial smack in the face by life (that loving and caring teacher I mentioned earlier). During a moment of insight, I realized why Linda kept reverting back to her old ways: she was the victim of her subconscious mind.

The subconscious mind is analogous to a computer that stores and runs programs. A computer will run a program only if it has been downloaded by a living, breathing, conscious human being. A computer can't and will not run a program that has not been downloaded. In like manner, our subconscious mind gets loaded up and programmed by all sorts of stimuli in our environment. What may seem spooky to some is that our subconscious mind can be programmed even without the participation of our conscious mind.

In other words, you download the programs in your *subconscious* mind, and your *conscious* brain opens up the program and runs it. If, for example, your parents promoted a poverty mind-set, you will be programmed with that mentality.

Linda was nothing more than a victim of her subconscious mind, which hosted hundreds of negative programs. So her conscious mind was busy running those very programs. This was evidenced by all the negativity that flowed from her lips. In a very real sense, she wasn't even aware of that negativity.

If we were to pry Linda's brain open and look at the programs that her subconscious mind was storing, we would see something similar to the following list. Keep in mind that I didn't just randomly write down these responses; they are from the conversations I had with her. I have phrased them differently so you can visualize her subconscious programming, but the original ideas behind her statements remain intact.

- "I am so busy, I don't have time to exercise."
- "I am so busy, I don't have time to prepare healthy food day in and day out. Heck, who does?"
- "I deserve to have sweet treats, given the stress I'm under."
- "I exercise so that I can eat what I want to."
- "I'm a foodie."
- "Nobody understands what I've been through, and I'm judged all too often."
- "My eating habits are the reflection of my lifestyle. I don't have any choice but to eat out frequently, and I don't have a choice to eat healthy because of the places where I'm forced to eat."

- "I come last because my family comes first."
- "I don't have the willpower or self-control to succeed."
- "Nobody in my shoes could or would succeed; it's impossible."
- "I'll get in shape someday."
- "I'll get my nutrition under control when my life slows down."
- "My life will slow down in the future."
- "I'll be happy when my life slows down."
- "Why does my life always throw me curve balls? Nobody else gets so many!"
- "I'm too emotionally upset to eat good at this point in my life."
- "Why do my genetics suck?"
- "Why can't I lose weight fast?"
- "Why do I hate healthy food, and why does cooking have to be so boring?"
- "Why is eating healthy so expensive, and why does a good meal take so long to prepare?"
- "Why can't my family—and especially my husband—support me more?"

Wow! What a revelation it was for me as I began to see what was happening to Linda on the *inside*! I was trying to fix her physical body, when what she needed was a "checkup from the neck up." This was a turning point in my career because I realized that in order for my clients to lead a healthy and fit lifestyle, they first needed to clear out the garbage programs that their subconscious minds were storing and that their conscious minds were parroting.

It is vitally important to remember that all Linda's storylines and programs were stored in her subconscious mind and her conscious mind was vocalizing and acting upon them.

The following principles will help you grasp the processes of the subconscious mind. Understanding the subconscious mind, at least at a basic level, is imperative so that we can later intervene and reprogram it consciously.

Laws and Principles of the Subconscious Mind

Subconscious principle 1: The subconscious governs 96 to 98 percent of all human behavior.

The poet William Wordsworth once brilliantly stated, "Habits rule the unreflecting herd." This one fact could change your life if you understand its significance. It means you will be ruled by your habits unless you make a *conscious* intervention. Consider the last time you actually *thought* about brushing your teeth. Did you think, *Take my brush in my hand. Apply toothpaste, and apply gentle pressure while creating circular motions. Move from tooth to tooth, and search for patches of plaque?* Of course not!

This seems absurd because we don't consciously brush our teeth; we do it subconsciously. Sure, we know at a conscious level that we're brushing our teeth, but the actual action and methodology is carried out mostly subconsciously. The same principle applies to driving to work every day, getting dressed and undressed, falling asleep every night, taking care of personal hygiene, and so forth.

The important point to remember is that your subconscious mind carries the programs that influence 96 to 98 percent of your behaviors. This encompasses nutritional habits, exercise habits, stressing habits, spiritual practices, and other avenues of your life that are paramount to your lifestyle.

Say, for example, that you consider yourself to have a sweet tooth, and you habitually drink a Coke each and every day. This behavior is the result of a subconscious program that simultaneously runs in your conscious mind; in other words, you just do it. If you're honest with yourself, you can identify numerous areas of your life that have been subjected to this insidious subconscious autopilot.

> The important point to remember is that your subconscious mind carries the programs that influence 96 to 98 percent of your behaviors. This encompasses nutritional habits, exercise habits, stressing habits, spiritual practices, and other avenues of your life that are paramount to your lifestyle.

This single principle was the game changer for Linda. Recall that I initially approached her program at a conscious level, when all her habits, tendencies, and behaviors were stemming from a subconscious level. When I switched my approach, her life started to change drastically.

Subconscious principle 2: The subconscious is programmed by external and internal programming.

When I was eight years old, I was a Cub Scout and enjoying my first trip to a local scouting camp. As I completed various workshops and activities, I felt like a true-blue Cub Scout, and my confidence soared. However, there was one particular merit badge station that has forever stood out from all others: the square-knot tying station, with Big Jason as the instructor.

Jason was a good-looking seventeen-year-old, and I was instantly impressed by his looks, knowledge, and charisma. (I admit that this was my first and last man crush.) Jason seemed to be having a great time teaching the class, and I was eager to be his next success story. I envisioned him praising me and extending his long arm upward for a high-five when I completed my task. My reality turned out to be quite different, and it took me off guard.

It was my turn to tie my knot, earn my badge, and impress Jason. But, in my haste to impress my hero, I froze. I couldn't seem to understand the sequence of a square knot, even after three or four demonstrations. Jason started out very friendly and understanding as he tried to help me, but soon he was visibly impatient with my inability to learn such a simple task.

What came next was instantly impressed onto my subconscious mind. With no patience left, Jason gave me a gentle slap upside my head and yelled in exasperation, "Man, how stupid can you be, kid?"

I was crushed. I had disappointed my newfound hero, and I wanted to crawl into a hole and die. The bright side of this story is the lesson that I learned many years later. I still have a phobia about knot tying, and I can't tie one to this very day. In essence, this experience served as an *external form* of subconscious conditioning because it came from an external source. I was told that I sucked at knot tying, and that's all my impressionable young mind needed to hear. The process of subconscious conditioning had begun, and my actions to this day have mirrored the belief that I suck at knot tying.

Now let's move on to *internal conditioning*. To properly understand the nature of internal conditioning, remember this axiom: "Where there is external conditioning, there is always a concomitant form of internal conditioning." To illustrate, consider the example of Jason and the square knots above. When he told me I "sucked" and that I was a "stupid kid," it came directly from an external source.

Since all forms of external conditioning lead to internal conditioning, when Jason belittled me, I began to ask myself questions: "Am I really a stupid kid?" and "Why am I bad at tying knots?" After receiving Jason's external conditioning and then subsequently asking myself disempowering questions, I began to form my own conclusions about my abilities. I continually replayed my conclusions in my head, and they led to *internal beliefs*. These beliefs directly influenced my behavior as a child and affected my confidence. As far as I was concerned, my conditioned beliefs were true.

> Where there is external conditioning, there is always
> a concomitant form of internal conditioning.

Linda had been actively and passively taking in external forms of conditioning her whole life. These conditioned beliefs were running around in her head: *You're fat. You're ugly. You can't do anything about your genetics.* They were nothing more than forms of external conditioning that she had internalized. The problem is that she internalized them to the point that she believed them to be true, and she never doubted them.

Subconscious principle 3: The subconscious is powerfully influenced by emotionalized experiences.

When you absorb various forms of environmental stimuli, your subconscious mind records them and then selectively places the most emotionally charged content front and center. To illustrate this, let me ask you this question: Where were you on the morning of April 16, 2001? Can't remember? Unless you had a birthday or an emotionally charged event take place on that day, you likely have no clue what went on.

In contrast, if I were to ask you where you were on the morning of September 11, 2001, you probably can tell me not only where you were but also what you were doing. In fact, you could probably tell me just about everything about that day in vivid detail. Why? Because the subconscious mind records events, thoughts, and experiences that are charged with emotion.

The same goes for your habits. Say, for example, you have a sugar addiction. Not only are you physiologically addicted to sugar, you are also *subconsciously* addicted. When you have your sugar fix, your brain ties that to something pleasurable.

In fact, some psychologists say that people aren't addicted food itself; rather, they're addicted to the experience and the *memory* it provides. Here's a simple example: If you go for chocolate when you're stressed, you're trying to escape your present moment of stress, which is unpleasant, and run to the more pleasurable memory that chocolate provides. As silly as it may sound, your mind has linked the chocolate to pleasure, and it has linked it as a stress reducer. This all equates to emotionalized memory making.

It's important to note that emotionally charged memories are wired into your subconscious mind, and they subsequently drive you to action— whether you're conscious of it or not. I leaned that Linda had endured many insulting comments as a youth from her parents and siblings. As a result, those comments and attitudes were burned into her subconscious mind.

The true problem was that she took all her external forms of conditioning and supercharged them with negative emotions. Once emotionalized, her subconscious mind began to cement those beliefs into her psyche, and her ability to make healthy choices was negatively influenced.

Subconscious principle 4: The subconscious operates in the now (present) and is impartial to opinions, judgments, and criticisms.

To better understand this principle, recall the last twenty-four hours of your life. What thoughts did you experience? How about your emotions? Were they positive, negative, or mixed? Now the question is, how did you recall these memories? The answer is that all your thoughts came from your conscious mind, not your subconscious mind.

You may be thinking about my previous example about 9/11, and saying, "Well, Griff, you just told me that the subconscious mind records the most emotionalized memories." And, yes, I did. Here is the distinction: the subconscious mind serves as a storehouse of information.

When 9/11 happened, it likely filled you with emotion. You then began to process it *consciously*, and a memory simultaneously planted at the *subconscious* level. When you recall that dreadful day, you do so from a conscious function. *In essence, you're reaching into your subconscious with your conscious mind and recalling what you're searching for.*

Your subconscious doesn't have the ability to analyze, recall, emotionalize, compare, contrast, make a judgment, search the past for memories, or contemplate the future. These are the functions of your conscious mind.

Your subconscious acts as a storage unit; as such, it simply houses your memories, habits, emotions, and traits, and plays them over and over like a computer program. The interesting thing about this program is that you aren't conscious of it running in the background. Your subconscious computer program has the power to influence your daily behaviors in a profound way if you don't consciously intercede.

We saw that Linda was using her conscious mind to reach into her subconscious mind (or her storage vault) and recall all the reasons, excuses, and alibis she needed to support her belief that she couldn't succeed in the long term. Essentially, she carried beliefs, attitudes, and negative emotional patterns that were self-defeating.

Your subconscious doesn't have the ability to analyze,
recall, emotionalize, compare, contrast, make a judgment,
search the past for memories, or contemplate the future.
These are the functions of your conscious mind.

All these self-defeating programs were stored and running silently—but powerfully—in her subconscious mind. Now follow me on this one: Using her *conscious* mind, she continually drew from these negative programs because she wasn't conscious of her self-limiting subconscious programming. This scenario presents the ultimate paradox in that she was consciously verbalizing programmed beliefs stored in her subconscious mind while simultaneously not being conscious that she was drawing from her subconscious mind.

Subconscious principle 5: Your subconscious mind connects you to your creative source

If that last paradox wasn't enough for you, consider this mind bender. Although your subconscious mind doesn't possess the ability to analyze, compare, contrast, or make judgment calls, it does have the ability to commune with your Source, as I discussed in chapter 1. Your Source is your creator (call it what you will: source energy, spirit, God, etc.), and it graciously grants you the ability to create anything in your life. This is part of your calling in life: to create whatever you are here to create. Remember this concept because I'll be coming back to it repeatedly.

The reason this carries such supreme relevance is because your Source contains infinite wisdom, and through your subconscious mind you tap into this infinite wellspring of knowledge. To illustrate my point, think of a time when you were hit by a sudden burst of intuition, a premonition, or a hunch that turned out not only to come true, but also to serve you. The logical question that follows is, where did it come from?

It certainly didn't come from your conscious mind, because you didn't have access to that knowledge up to that point in your life. It had to come from somewhere. That somewhere was your Source, which communicates with you through your subconscious mind.

Yes, this is a mind-bending idea, and there is no science to back it up. Yet some of the greatest leaders and philosophers of our day have acknowledged this function of the subconscious mind, and if you're honest with yourself, I'm sure you realize you've had these moments.

So, here you are, reading a book about eliminating your excuses, and here I am, going off and speaking about your Source, Universe, God. Why? I hope you already know the answer to this question; if not, rest assured that I'll clarify it perfectly in the next few chapters.

Linda had forgotten that she had an unlimited capacity to create her own life and to succeed in her undertakings. She could not escape the negative conditioning (both internal and external) that had been stored in her subconscious mind. In essence, she had forgotten her divine potential and instead hung on to her conditioned belief that she was a victim of external circumstances. She began to make progress only when she reconnected with her spiritual Source through her subconscious mind.

Subconscious principle 6: You program your subconscious mind with your conscious mind

According to the first principle, your conscious mind is responsible for only 2 to 4 percent of all your habitual behavior. Did you catch that? Only 2 to 4 percent! Here is where the irony gets thick. *You can change your existing subconscious programming only through conscious intervention.* Remember your subconscious mind can only absorb information fed to it through your environment at both a conscious and a subconscious level.

So what does this mean for your life? You're being steered by your subconscious mind via its faulty programming into habits that you'd rather leave behind. It means you get frustrated because you can't seem to break your habits. You must intervene at a conscious level and repeat your conscious efforts until your subconscious is reprogrammed.

Once I understood these life-changing principles and saw them work in my own life, I was able to see why I wasn't able to help Linda change her life. With these new tools, I hope to help you reprogram your brain—and therefore your life. See you in the next chapter!

CHAPTER 3

BECOME AWARE OF YOUR CONDITIONED INNER WORLDVIEW

Reality as You See It, Not as It Is

Perception is reality.
—Lee Atwater

When I was a teenager, I was lucky to have several close friends, especially Jason and Michael. Both of these guys were jokers; they constantly made fun of everyone and everything. While I thought they were hilarious at the time, I was often the target of their jokes. Specifically, they loved to tease me about my inability to attract women, make money, be cool, play sports, and a host of other things that were important to me at the time.

For example, one night they were teasing me about the upcoming homecoming dance. I can still remember Michael predicting how his perfect night would go: "There I am with the homecoming queen, pulling up to the dance in my cousin's Camaro."

Jason would then add to the picture. "There I am, pulling up with the head cheerleader by my side."

Then, laughing, they described my night at the dance: "Here comes Griff, being dropped off by Mommy and Daddy and *looking* for a date." Yes, they would laugh and brag at my expense. To go even further, they predicted how much money they would make later in life while saying I would drive a 1979 Ford Pinto into my late fifties.

The harassing and heckling was all in teenage fun, and I assure you they weren't trying to be mean or vindictive. Rather, they were doing what teenagers do best: pumping up their developing egos by tearing others down.

In the moment, I laughed and went along with their antics. I never considered that my mind was being subjected subtly to their unintentional conditioning. After hearing such stories day after day and year after year, I began to believe that I was indeed "the dumb one" in the group, and I began to act that way.

I also began to believe that I was the ugly duckling. I became shy and avoided good-looking women at all costs. I simply thought they were out of my league and I wasn't worthy. In my three years of high school, I never asked a girl out. I could always be found on the sidelines, watching in envy as Jason and Michael took their dates to all the dances and enjoyed many dates on Friday nights. In essence, the stories of me "looking for a date" were coming true.

It's apparent why I became the shy guy who never asked a girl out or had the guts to attend a dance. I was the victim of mental conditioning, but that itself wasn't the problem. My problem was that I actually *believed* my friends' seemingly innocuous slander.

Once we begin to believe self-limiting notions, they begin to inform our daily lives. They appear as excuses, justifications, and rationalizations for our shortcomings. Given time and repetition, these belief systems become our reality, and we enter a vicious cycle in which our daily actions begin to reinforce our newfound beliefs.

This concept is illustrated in the diagram below, which I designed after reading numerous books on psychology and personal development and after seeing it play out repeatedly in my own life. I have also seen it in the lives of my clients for the past fifteen years.

I have named the diagram the Perceived Reality Model for Self-Sabotage simply because it shows that deeply held perceptions and beliefs create our inner reality. In other words, your inner reality is your personal belief system based on your core values. *These beliefs and values continually drive you to act, and these actions led you to your current reality.*

PERCEPTION REALITY MODEL FOR
SELF SABOTAGE

STAGE #1 –
EARLY YEARS

- No Conditioning
- No Self Limiting Beliefs
- Desire = Action
- Self Confidence = 100%

STAGE #2 –
"Conditioning" Begins

- Told what we are good / bad at
- Expectations placed upon us
- Conditioning is from internal and external sources
- Conditioning is Emotionalized

STAGE #3 –
New Self-Limiting Beliefs Formed

- Because conditioning is emotionalized we start to believe it.
- Beliefs are impressed onto the subconscious mind
- Reinforcements begins with "self-talk"

STAGE #4 –
Belief = Action

- Beliefs and actions align
- Action is the byproduct
- Lifestyle becomes a mirror of beliefs
- Beliefs are self-defeating / limiting

STAGE #5 –
New Perceived Reality

- Because our beliefs are "true" we take it as reality
- Our continued actions confirm our "reality"

Current Results
=
Current Lifestyle / Habits

Note: This is completely opposite of Stage #1 if you are failing in an area of your life.

Let's discuss how you became who you are and why you believe what you believe. Using my own story as an example, let's start in stage 1 of this model.

Stage 1: The Early Years

During the first two years of my life, I didn't experience a large amount of conditioning from myself (internal) or from others (external). At that age, if I wanted something, I simply went and got it. For example, my father loves to remind me about the time my family was intently watching a Utah Jazz game during overtime. I was only two years old, and I saw a toy on top of the TV. I was too short to get the toy, but I was determined to get up there, come hell or high water.

Stubbornly, I searched the room until I found a chair stashed in a corner for decorative purposes. In two seconds flat, I darted for the chair and began to drag that sucker in front of my father's big TV set. I got up onto the chair, stretched out my short little body, and grabbed the toy, despite the annoyed requests from my father to get out of the way.

Now let's examine my game-interrupting behavior a bit closer.

Here is what I *did*: I got my toy.

Here is what I *did not do:* I didn't question myself. I didn't have an internal dialogue with myself like, *Gee, I sure wish I could have that toy, but unfortunately Dad is watching TV, and I want to be courteous to him by allowing him to have this moment uninterrupted.* Furthermore, I didn't reason, *Wow, that toy is really far up there, and I don't think I have the stomach to put forth all the effort needed to get it.* I didn't think, *Maybe I'll try some other time when I've grown a few more inches and when I'm more prepared.*

Look at the difference between the two scenarios. When we aren't limited by our own conditioned beliefs, we act. In other words:

Desire = Action

I wanted my toy. Period. Because I wanted it, I got it. Period. My self-confidence was 100 percent, and I had no self-limiting conditioned beliefs holding me back

> If you labor under a state of mind filled with excuses, reasons, and justifications for not acting on your desires, know— without a doubt—that it is in direct contrast to the original state that you were born into: the state of your Higher Self.

Now let's think about what this means. Recall a time when you wanted something, such as a college degree, a date with a special someone, or to run a marathon, but you ended up talking yourself out of it. You more than likely came up with myriad reasons, justifications, and excuses that prevented you from achieving your goal.

I've done this multiple times, and I know you have too. Remember this: If you labor under a state of mind filled with excuses, reasons, and justifications for not acting on your desires, know—without a doubt—that it is in direct contrast to the original state that you were born into: the state of your Higher Self.

As you continued to grow up, and your conditioning lessons intensified, you were introduced into stage 2.

Stage 2: Conditioning Begins

From a very early age, the process of conditioning took root in your life. You were told what you were good at, and you were told what you were bad at. These messages could have come in direct and indirect ways, but it didn't matter, because your subconscious mind was soaking it in like a sponge.

It is important to know that conditioning can take many forms, such as the following:

- religious
- political

- educational expectations
- nutritional habits and expectations
- exercise habits and expectations
- athletic preferences and expectations
- the importance of being popular as a kid
- keeping up with the Joneses as an adult
- what is realistic or not realistic for you to achieve
- your genetic limitations
- your mental limitations or abilities (depending on the opinions of parents, teachers, etc.)
- conditioning based on test scores such as the SAT and ACT (you're smart or stupid based on the score)
- conditioning based on statements or phrases uttered by friends, family, or classmates, such as "you're a cute kid" or "you're a four-eyed freckle-faced stepchild"
- parental expectations in *any* area of life
- family expectations
- societal expectations

These are a few of the classic forms of conditioning that you were likely exposed to as a child. It's also a fact that you're continually exposed to the conditioning on a daily basis as an adult, even though it may take different forms. Jason and Michael's conditioning affected my mind and therefore my actions for the majority of my teenage years up until my midtwenties. Then I began to study the mind and how it works. I am now aware of the power and the danger of conditioning, and I've undone the programs that dictated my confidence and self-limiting actions for so many years.

> The most powerful form of conditioning is that
> which is emotionalized and repeated.

The final point to remember for phase 2 of this model is this: the most powerful form of conditioning is that which is *emotionalized and repeated.* For example, when I was the butt of Jason and Michael's jokes every day, it bred a very powerful form of subconscious conditioning that created negative emotions in my being. The combination of emotion and repetition can be either advantageous or highly destructive to your habitual way of thinking and acting. This leads us straight into stage 3.

Stage 3: New Self-Limiting Belief Formed

When a thought, belief, or attitude has been repeated and/or emotionalized over time, it becomes deeply internalized. I began to believe everything that Jason and Michael said to me, and it became part of my inner reality. When I say "inner reality," I'm referring to a subconscious mind that has been programmed by external thoughts, beliefs, and attitudes.

Remember that the process of conditioning is *always* in play. Conditioning is neutral in that it can be either advantageous or destructive. Without awareness of this process, it is tempting to utter self-justifying statements such as, "This is just the way I am" or "This is my nature." In fact, your current reality is nothing more than the product of all the conditioning of your life.

Negative beliefs are dangerous because they lead to negative self-talk. Every day, you have conversations in your mind. We *all* do! Having these conversations is not only normal, it's also human nature. The problem is when we repeat negative conditioning, such as "I'm a loser" or "I will always be overweight." This destructive form of self-talk leads you directly into stage 4.

Stage 4: Belief Equals Action

After I received my conditioning from Jason and Michael (stage 2) and began believing it at a subconscious level (stage 3), I began to *act* on it. I shied away from the cute girls, thinking I was an ugly schmuck—or at least a lesser form of a human being—because I was conditioned to believe that. The point to remember here is that my beliefs led to action. My inner reality told me that I was unworthy of the opposite sex, and my actions followed suit.

I would often form a crush on a girl but then shy away from her if she threw a favorable look in my direction. As far as I was concerned, I was unworthy of women and was a nuisance in their eyes. With these beliefs etched into my skull, I reasoned that I should be respectful of them by not look at them or speak to them. The problem was that my beliefs were self-defeating in nature, and they directly influenced my actions.

> Your inner reality is your personal belief system based on your core values. These beliefs and values continually drive you to act, and these actions led you to your current reality.

What I'm about to say is not for the faint of heart, but it needs to be said. If you're honest with yourself, you will find many active examples of this stage in your own life. If you're overweight, you may have been conditioned to believe that your genetics are stacked against you so you're doomed to have a hard time losing weight. Although this belief may contain an *element* of truth, it is far from reality, and it directly influences your actions.

You may have started a new fitness program only to crash and burn two weeks into it because your subconscious "inner reality" began to assert its conditioned beliefs in your conscious mind. It practically yelled phrases: "You're fat, and you will always be fat—so just give up!" or "You don't have enough time for exercise." Again, if you're honest with yourself, you'll find that your beliefs directly influence your actions.

Please allow me to illustrate my point. If you believe you don't have time for exercise or good nutrition, you don't because you won't make the time. If you believe that you're always going to be fat, why not have another doughnut? If your doctor has told you that you have a predisposition toward a weight problem, why try? If you hate exercising and it stresses you out, how can you possibly do it? If you don't have enough energy for exercise, you can't do it, right?

If you believe that you don't have time for exercise or good nutrition, you don't because you won't make the time. If you believe that you're always going to be fat, why not have another doughnut?

When you begin to act on your faulty beliefs, they lead you directly into the final stage of reality: stage 5.

Stage 5: New Perceived Reality

Notice the wording of this stage. In particular, notice one key word: *perceived*. When you enter this stage of conditioning, you perceive your world according to the conditioning you've been subjected to.

Here is a simplified diagram that nicely depicts what we discussed above:

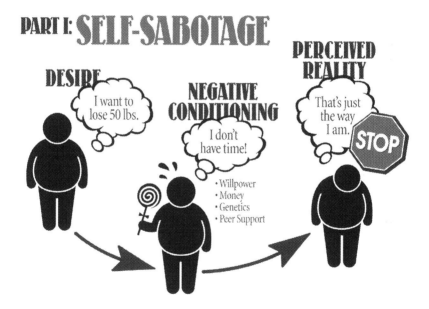

I knew a family of doctors in California who were convinced they were in the one true profession. They wholeheartedly believed that to be a successful person, one had to be a doctor, period. They even voiced this opinion directly to me, knowing I was, indeed, not a doctor. They had no problems uttering this offensive garble because they were so convinced, or conditioned, to believe what they were spewing.

In short, that was their perceived reality, and it didn't make a lick of difference what anybody thought of them, because they were right in their own mind—and that was all that mattered. I once observed them saying this to a successful businessperson who made three times the amount of money they did. But it didn't change their opinion of him, because their inner reality dictated that being a doctor was the *only* way to be successful.

Just as this family of doctors lived in its own little fantasyland, we create perceived realities that can either help or harm our personal development. If what we believe to be realities are negative and pessimistic, we will be inclined to act on those realities.

I have another story that perfectly depicts the power of conditioning and how it affects one's life. As I previously mentioned, Jason and Michael were experts in creating stories that downplayed my ability and potential as a human being. I was told that I would never make money, attract a person of the opposite sex, or make anything of myself. This, in and of itself, was life changing for me in a negative way. Fortunately, I was blessed with an eye-opening moment that gave me my first glimpse into the power of mental conditioning.

> Remember that the process of conditioning is always in play. Conditioning is neutral in that it can be advantageous or destructive. Without awareness of this process, it is tempting to utter self-justifying statements such as, "This is just the way I am" or "This is my nature." In fact, your current reality is nothing more than the gross product of all the collective conditioning of your life.

It all began in eighth-grade English class. It was the first day of school, and I launched into my customary practice of scanning the classroom for pretty girls—or chicks, as we referred them in the early nineties. My rotating head came to a standstill when my eyes fell upon Abby Buress, whose name has been changed to protect my eighth-grade love. Something about her grabbed my attention and commanded my respect. She had long blonde hair, and when she got up to sharpen her pencil, I took my first look at her legs and about fell off my chair. She was gorgeous!

For the better part of my eighth-grade year, I made it a regular practice to sneak a peek at Abby. I was both exhilarated and terrified—exhilarated because I would fantasize about her looking at me or having a friend come up and tell me that she liked me, but terrified because I was conditioned by my buddies to believe that she was out of my league and that I wasn't capable of scoring a girl like that. I went through my year never once speaking to her.

As my ninth-grade year commenced, I was lucky enough to have Abby in yet another one of my classes. The only difference from the year before is that she caught me looking at her a few times. These were awkward moments because I knew I had been busted. Even so, I tried to pull the ole quick glance to the opposite direction, which failed miserably. I still couldn't muster up the courage to speak to her. After all, my inner reality, or perceived reality, dictated that I was not worthy of such a girl.

Near the end of my sophomore year, I found myself in yet another class with Abby, but nothing changed as far as my inner beliefs were concerned. What did change was what to me was a sign from God: assigned seating! I experienced the most terrifying yet exhilarating moment of my life as I was assigned to sit directly next to the one-and-only Abby.

I remember having a hard time breathing normally as she sat next to me. I even recall her having bad breath, but it didn't matter, because it was Abby, the girl who had found her way into many of my teenage dreams. And she was sitting next to me for the rest of the semester. *Score!*

One of my saving graces was having one of my best friends sitting in back of me. This eased the pressure to speak to Abby, because if I was talking to my friend, by definition I couldn't speak to Abby. The irony of the situation is that I desperately wanted to speak to her and tell her that I liked her, but I couldn't overcome my fears. My subconscious mind was filled with reasons why she could never return my attention.

Three weeks into the class, I experienced a pleasant but unexpected shock. Abby turned to me, and said, "So, how are you doing, Griff?" My first response was a gasp. I literally made a quiet gasping noise because this wasn't supposed to be happening. My subconscious programming had specifically told me that Abby would never speak to me, because she was out of my league. What was happening? Was I dreaming?

Nope. With a grin on her face, she redoubled and asked politely again, "How are you doing?"

I knew it was real that time, not just a story spun out of the fantasy department of my imagination. I somehow managed to reply, "Great, Abby. How are you?"

What followed was a five-minute surface conversation that stayed in my dreams for the next two weeks straight. Abby was all I could think about. I was obsessed. I spoke to her a few times after that and even made her laugh half a dozen times. What came next was predictable. My subconscious programming kicked in and reminded me that she was out of my league and that I shouldn't have any foolish expectations of her actually liking me.

In February 1995, on a chilly morning, my teenage life changed forever. I strolled into class a little bit late and found my way to my seat. To my everlasting surprise and delight, I was greeted by Abby with a grin on her face as she uttered a suspenseful statement: "I'm glad you made it to class, tardy boy! I have a question to ask you after class." I was perplexed. What could her question possibly be?

After what seemed to be a week, the bell rang, and class was dismissed. Abby gathered her books, looked straight into my eyes with a burning intensity, and asked, "Have you been asked to the Senior Cotillion yet?"

I searched for the breath and lung stamina to utter the phrase, "Yes, I mean *no!*"

She laughed and said, "Well, then, it's a date, right?"

Needless to say, I was shocked beyond belief and floated on cloud nine for the next year. More importantly, I learned a very powerful and life-changing lesson that has influenced my thinking ever since that day of glory. I learned that my mind lied to me. All the conditioning that I'd received from Jason and Michael was nonsense. All the external and internal conditioning that I'd esteemed as gospel was a fairy tale housed in my subconscious mind.

What I learned is this: A conditioned mind is a powerful mind that has the ability to influence belief. I learned that belief directly influences action. And ultimately I learned that I have the power to change my deeply held, self-defeating, habitual thoughts. I learned that I am more capable than my conditioned mind had given me credit for.

Indeed, my perceived reality wasn't reality. In the next chapter, I'll introduce you to the steps that you can take to change your inner realities and conditioned beliefs that are keeping you motionless and frustrated. Now it's time to take a walk and clear your conditioned mind so we can rock-and-roll in the next chapter.

CHAPTER 4

CREATING A NEW AND
EXCITING WORLDVIEW

Aligning Your Conditioned Mind with the Desires of Your Heart

The reflection of the current social paradigm tells us
we are largely determined by conditioning and conditions.
—Stephen R. Covey, *The 7 Habits of Highly Effective
People: Powerful Lessons in Personal Change*

The previous chapters explored the ways direct and indirect conditioning create your habits and shapes your reality. For example, if you're addicted to food, you likely have been conditioned a certain way about food and the way it affects your decisions. At this moment, you likely have certain self-defeating beliefs that lead to unwanted negative behavior.

In this chapter, you'll learn how to convert this negative conditioning into positive energy. It is precisely this positive energy that will help you redefine who you are. Once you redefine yourself according to your terms, the sky is the limit. I'm excited, so let's get right to it.

In the previous chapter, I took you step-by-step through the Perceived Reality Model and used myself as an example. Now I want to take you through the steps again, but this time, I'll share something very powerful with you. You are about to learn how you can *consciously* intervene and

proactively condition your mind according to the desires of your heart—
the desires that previously evaded you.

The following diagram is not the same as the self-sabotage depicted in
the last chapter. Take a look at it, and I'll take you through a step-by-step
breakdown afterward. Take note of the very subtle changes that differentiate
the Self-Empowerment Model from the Sabotage Model.

PERCEPTION REALITY MODEL FOR
SELF EMPOWERMENT

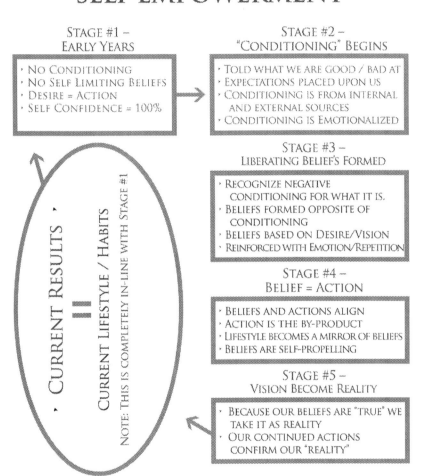

STAGE #1 –
EARLY YEARS

- No Conditioning
- No Self Limiting Beliefs
- Desire = Action
- Self Confidence = 100%

STAGE #2 –
"Conditioning" Begins

- Told what we are good / bad at
- Expectations placed upon us
- Conditioning is from internal and external sources
- Conditioning is Emotionalized

STAGE #3 –
Liberating Belief's Formed

- Recognize negative conditioning for what it is.
- Beliefs formed opposite of conditioning
- Beliefs based on Desire/Vision
- Reinforced with Emotion/Repetition

STAGE #4 –
Belief = Action

- Beliefs and actions align
- Action is the by-product
- Lifestyle becomes a mirror of beliefs
- Beliefs are self-propelling

STAGE #5 –
Vision Become Reality

- Because our beliefs are "true" we take it as reality
- Our continued actions confirm our "reality"

Current Results = Current Lifestyle / Habits

Note: This is completely in-line with Stage #1

Stage 1: *The Early Years*

Nothing changes here. See the previous chapter for a complete description of this stage.

Stage 2: *Conditioning Begins*

Ditto here! We all experience good and bad forms of conditioning. Nobody is exempt from this. This stage is the same as in the first model in the previous chapter. Without a doubt, you have and will experience all sorts of conditioning that subtly or aggressively influences the way you see yourself and the world around you.

Stage 3: *New Self-Liberating Beliefs Formed*

This is where it gets good because this stage is the game changer. It is the stage where you use your God-given abilities to create positive internal conditioning through self-will and self-awareness. In my estimation, there's nothing more powerful than this stage.

> When you can differentiate the desires of your heart from
> the conditioned stories of your mind, you will be well on
> your way to achieving your goals. It is all about awareness.

This stage has three steps that are imperative to initiating the process of self-conditioning.

1. *You must become aware of the negative or self-limiting conditioning.*

I discussed how a girl named Abby helped me become aware of negative conditioning in my life. Specifically, when she asked me to the dance, I suddenly realized that the negative things I had believed about myself were not the truth at all. In your case, you can proactively investigate your own negative conditioning. To get you started in the right direction, consider the following examples:

- "I don't have time to exercise."
- "I'm too ugly to care about myself."
- "I don't have the discipline to eat healthy foods for a long period."
- "My genetics limit what I can be anyway, so why should I care?"

This is just a small sample of the self-limiting conditioning that your mind might have come to accept as fact. This step dictates that you first recognize conditioning for what it is: nothing more than beliefs that are preventing you from reaching your goals.

When you recognize that your beliefs are largely a result of internal and external forms of conditioning, magic begins to happen. Now you can replace your negative conditioning with the desires of your *heart*. The following are examples of mind stories, which are those stories you tell yourself that are based on the conditioned beliefs floating around in your head. I will then contrast these mind stories to the desires of your heart, which will illustrate the difference between the two.

Desire of your heart: "I want to lose fifty pounds and look sexy for my spouse again."

Mind story: "I've tried to lose fifty pounds before, and I know what to expect: lose ten or twenty pounds, feel deprived, get angry and frustrated, eat more, gain weight back, and start process over again."

Desire of your heart: "I want to exercise for thirty minutes a day."

Mind story: "I'm so busy at this time in my life, I don't think I can make the time for exercise. I'll try, but if it doesn't work out, I'll have to try again when life slows down."

Desire of your heart: "I want to eat less sugar."

Mind story: "I'm a sugar addict, and I can't help myself! If I see sugar, I eat it. Even if I keep it out of my house, I'm bound to run into it at work, at church, or with friends, so why even try? It really isn't fair that I'm addicted to sugar and that all the food that tastes good just happens to be bad for me."

Desire of your heart: "I want to feel confident in my own body again."

Mind story: "I don't deserve to feel confident, given my lack of performance in the past. Every time I try to accomplish something, I sabotage myself and end up at square one. So, from here on out, I am not going to set myself up for failure."

Desire of your heart: "I want to feel young and full of energy again!"

Mind story: "I'm too old to change the way I feel. Let's face it: I'm over the hill, so I might as well tone it down a notch and start acting my age. High expectations are a recipe for disaster, and I need to be mature enough to realize this."

Desire of your heart: "I want to run a marathon (or fill in your personal physical goal here)."

Mind story: "Although I really want to run a marathon, I have to remind myself that I don't have time to train for one. And I don't have the physical ability to run that distance without killing myself."

These are just a few of the numerous mind stories that we entertain and excuse ourselves with. Please, please, *please* remember that your mind stories are nothing more than the conditioned programming of your subconscious mind. When you can differentiate the desires of your heart from the conditioned stories of your mind, you will be well on your way to achieving your goals. It is all about *awareness*.

Once I became aware that Jason and Michael were the source of my conditioned beliefs and that my beliefs were nothing more than mind stories, I was able to replace negative conditioning with the desires of my heart, which led me into the next step.

2. You must form beliefs that are the opposite of your negative conditioning, thereby replacing them with the more desirable intentions of your heart.

Take a deep breath because this is the easiest of the three steps. In the last step, you became aware of your limiting beliefs. Now that you're aware them, you have the power to replace those SOBs with the desirable intentions of your heart. In my case, once I learned that Abby liked me, I allowed the desires of my heart to take hold.

To further illustrate my personal example, I began to replace my conditioned beliefs created by Jason and Michael with beliefs like the following:

"I'm good-looking, and girls like me."

"I'm strong and attractive to women."

"I can be myself because women like me for who I am."

These and many other thoughts started to flood my mind. At first I felt guilty about them, but I didn't care because my Higher Self was calling, and the proof was in the pudding. I ran with my newly formed beliefs, and I have never looked back. It feels good to replace old damaging thoughts with those that lift you to a new level of happiness and confidence.

This will start you on the path to rewiring your brain—and I don't say *rewiring* in the figurative sense. When you begin to challenge your old beliefs and *replace* them, you're literally rewiring the neurons in your brain. How cool is that! The only problem is that your initial barrage of positive thinking will be short-lived and sabotaged by your subconscious mind if you don't take the final step.

3. Your newly created beliefs must be reinforced with repetition and emotion.

Our brains have often been likened to computers. Our physical brain is the hardware. It has a physical shape and the capacity to hold data that we allow to be stored in it. Our subconscious mind can be likened to software. Any software can be consciously or unconsciously downloaded. In the same way, you can be programmed without your conscious consent if you don't add the filter of awareness to your conscious mind.

Your brain can have good or bad software installed in it. The good software is the desires of your heart, and the bad software is the negative form of conditioning, which we previously discussed.

Our conscious mind can easily be likened to the RAM (random access memory or working memory) of a computer. Your subconscious mind houses your beliefs, habits of thought, and proclivities, acting like the software of your brain. For example, if you habitually think, *I am never on time*, this belief is housed in the software program of your subconscious mind, which runs 24-7 in the background of your brain.

Now, hang in there with me on this next point, because it can be a little tricky—but it is very important to understand. Just because your subconscious mind houses your beliefs, habits of thought, and proclivities in a software package doesn't mean it *runs* the software. That's the job of your conscious mind.

Your conscious mind extracts from your subconscious mind the thoughts, desires, proclivities, and tendencies that your subconscious mind is housing. In other words, your subconscious mind houses the software, and your conscious mind runs it. Let's break this down using our previous example.

If your subconscious mind has the software downloaded, and the program says, "I'm never on time," it's running that program in your brain 24-7. So when you have to be somewhere on time, you have the thought, *I'm never on time*, which comes from your conscious mind only after it has accessed it from your subconscious mind.

If all this seems complicated, read this section over a few times until it makes sense. This is crucial to understand if you're going to purge yourself of excuse making and other forms of negative conditioning. It's really not that complicated once you understand the basic principles of the conscious and subconscious mind.

You may be asking at this point, "Griff, what does your little computer analogy have to do with reinforcing a new belief with repetition and emotion?" Great question! Your subconscious mind is full of different software programs that are detrimental to your success, so you must actively replace them with new ones. You can do this by taking the new beliefs in step 2 and repeating them day in and day out with emotion and passion.

For example, if you believe that you're addicted to sugar, you can replace that belief with the following: "I am in complete control of my sugar intake, and I abide by my own limits." When you say this, you must say it as though you've already achieved your goal, and you must say it with emotion and passion. I'll go over this in more detail in the next chapter.

In essence, you're rewiring your brain to think in different and more productive ways. If you're thinking this is hocus-pocus, just refer back to the Perceived Reality Model in the previous chapter. Remember any conditioned belief was formed in the same way: with repetition and emotion. Here you're simply using your conscious faculties to override the preexisting conditioning of your subconscious mind, which leads us to the next stages of the Perceived Reality Model:

Stage 4: New Self-Liberating Beliefs Form

The only element that changes here is that your newly created beliefs are self-propelling rather than self-sabotaging. These beliefs literally propel you toward your goal at an unprecedented rate. This is in stark contrast to your previously beliefs, which actively held you back from your goals.

Remember that all action is driven by belief. This is the stage where magic happens because you have formed new, affirmative, and empowering beliefs. Simply put, once you believe these, you begin to act on them and improve your life.

Stage 5: New Vision Becomes Reality

At this point, your beliefs are *true* as far as your subconscious and conscious mind are concerned. When I reached this point with Abby, my whole demeanor changed because I *knew* I was the man. Although I never voiced this audibly, I was sure of it in my mind, and I have never doubted it since. Let me assure you that my new self-imposed conditioning wasn't that of a conceited nature, but rather of confidence.

Your goal is to be 100 percent confident in your ability to achieve the desires of your heart.

When you finally reach this stage, your actions will continue to reinforce your beliefs. I continued to speak to girls whenever I wanted, and my fears continued to diminish. In essence, my continued action reinforced my new reality, the reality I had been seeking all along.

Using the sugar addict example, once you reach this stage, you are no longer a sugar addict in your mind. Instead, you have proactively replaced it with an empowering belief that you are in complete control of your sugar intake; you set your own limits. With your newly formed belief, your actions continually mirror the belief and thereby lead you into making wise nutritional choices.

Does this sound like magic? Hardly! This science of the mind has been around for decades, and now you're aware of it and can apply it.

Now that I'm done explaining the model, I want to make a very powerful point. If you look at the lower left-hand portion of the diagram at the beginning of the chapter, you will notice that you have now drastically altered the results of your life. You've changed your subconscious and conscious beliefs and can now create the lifestyle you desire.

Ironically, in this stage you're completely in line with stage 1—where you began! This does *not* mean you have digressed, but rather that you have shed yourself of your limiting beliefs, and you are 100 percent confident in your ability to succeed. Remember my example of getting in front of my father's TV while he was watching the basketball game so I could get my toy? I was in a state of nonconditioned beliefs, and my desire equaled action. In this stage, you have returned to your original nature, where desire leads to action because you don't have layers of conditioned beliefs holding you back.

You must rid yourself of the negative conditioning. Period. Remember in this stage you're operating from your Highest Self—the part of you that knows no limits. The following diagram nicely summarizes the revised Perception Reality Model.

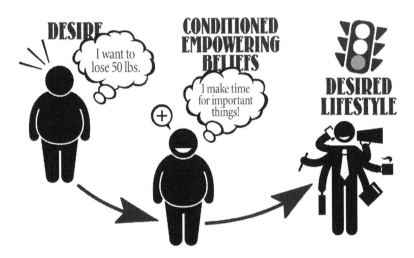

Here is what you get after you recondition your mind and operate from your Highest Self:

Desire = Action

Action = Results

Results = Desired lifestyle

Summary

First, become *consciously* aware of your negative conditioning. Remember that the negative voices in your head and the accompanying mind stories come from your conditioned subconscious mind. Understand that you have the power to change those conditioned beliefs and stories this moment—not after New Year's or three weeks prior to your high school reunion. Right *now*!

Second, you must *consciously* replace your negative conditioned beliefs with beliefs based on the desires of your heart. So instead of thinking, *I am a chocoholic*, you will replace it with this: *I am in complete control of what goes into my mouth at any time and under any circumstance.*

In the beginning of this book, you were given a comprehensive action assignments that you can use to replace and eliminate negative conditioning.

*Third, a*dd passion, emotion, and conviction while mentally rehearsing and implementing your new beliefs.

I hope you're excited to implement the themes of this chapter in your life, for they are truly life-changing. Now it's time to roll on to learn about the most negative form of conditioning known to humankind.

CHAPTER 5

Excused from Health and Fitness

Liberating Yourself from the Bondage of Excuses

*An excuse is nothing more than an option out
of the life that you would like to live.*
—Wayne W. Dyer

In the 1998 hit movie *The Truman Show,* Truman is living what he thinks is a normal and happy life. Unbeknownst to him, he is really an actor in a reality TV show that depicts his life in real time for viewers to see. In Truman's mind, he is living in the real world and is just as normal as all his friends, who are actually actors and actresses.

At the climatic end of the movie, Truman realizes that something isn't right and tries to escape the conspiracy. In his attempt to flee his environment, he finally finds "the open" and makes his move—only to find a wall. Truman is crushed as he learns that his entire life and everything that he valued in it was nothing more than fiction.

With striking similarity, many of us believe today that we are living in the real world when we are actually living in a world created by the beliefs that we unconsciously allow into our minds. As mentioned in the previous chapter, we create our own reality. In this chapter, you'll learn a form of conditioning that will suck the very life out of your dreams, hopes, and goals. You will also learn the tried-and-true principles of reversing this tyrannical form of conditioning.

The conditioning I speak of is excuse making. Make no mistake, we *all* make excuses, and we all suffer the consequences of so doing. For more on this subject, I highly recommend that you purchase *Excuses Begone* by Dr. Wayne W. Dyer and read it cover to cover multiple times throughout your life.

"*Dam*" Excuses!

I'm always amazed when I drive by a reservoir and see a dam holding back millions of gallons of water. The amount of potential energy in the restrained water is almost inconceivable. It's amazing that just a slab of cement and steel—with just a fraction of the mass of the water—can hold back all that energy.

As I mentioned earlier, I'm convinced that the most "damming" form of conditioning is that of excuse making. We all have hopes, dreams, goals, and aspirations that ignite our passions and inspire us. There is a part of our soul that *knows* it's possible to reach the hope, the dream, the goal, or the aspiration that we so desperately seek. I will refer to this part of our nature as our *Highest* Self.

When life becomes chaotic, it's easy to forget about your Higher Self. When this happens, as it assuredly will, you'll find a side of you that I call your Deceived Self. I've named this part of your being this way because it truly deceives you into thinking that you aren't capable of accomplishing the desires of your heart. It is the proverbial dam that stands between you and the desires of your heart.

Your Deceived Self would have you believe the following:

- I am limited.
- I need to have reasonable expectations.
- My past is indicative of my future.

- I lack time.
- I lack ability.
- It isn't the right time of life for me to act on my desires.
- I don't have enough external support from my family and friends.
- I lack drive and desire.
- It's just the way I am.
- It's how God made me!
- I am not cut out for my goals, and I'm incapable of achieving the desires of my heart.
- I'm genetically limited.
- My life is too busy.
- I'm too stressed out to improve myself.

This is just a small sample of what your Deceived Self would have you believe, but the dirty little secret is that these are nothing more than excuses. Yes, excuses! If you're now tempted to think, *Excuses! Well, excuses or not, this is my life!* I invite you understand what the Deceived Self does to your original nature and how it can limit your limitless potential. To accomplish this, let's talk a little more about your original nature.

Your Original Nature

In stage 1 of the Perception Reality Model that I presented in the last chapter, there was no conditioning, which means you haven't been shackled by the limitations of conditioned thinking. As we age, we become accustomed to multiple forms of conditioning that influence our thinking, which in turn influences our actions. Excuses are, without question, the worst form of mental conditioning because they take us into stage 6 of the Perception Reality Model. To give you a refresher, this is where we believe our excuses to be true.

When we enter this stage of conditioning, we forget a precious truth: we are created from a Source that doesn't know what excuses are. Most of us would agree that we come from a higher power, although we may not agree on the name of that source (God, Christ, Universe, Source, Spirit, etc.). In the context of our discussion, the title is meaningless, so I'll use the terms Source or God because it is universal in nature, and it pertains to whatever you choose to believe.

As a mental exercise, imagine your Source making excuses. If you agree that your Source created you, and you further agree that it created all life, I invite you to imagine your Source making excuses when the going gets tough. Can you imagine under any circumstance God making excuses like the following?

- "I would really like to create a new world today, but I have too much to do. I will have to put it off for a while until I have the time."
- "I would like to bless your life today, my child, but I have too many people asking for things, so you'll just have to wait."
- "I'm lacking the strength to be God today, so I think I'll just be lazy and get back on the wagon tomorrow."

That these statements could be made by your all-knowing, all-caring Source is incomprehensible, and if you are a person of faith, it may be reprehensible to entertain such nonsense. I, for one, can't imagine a God making any form of excuse for any reason, because it isn't possible. If you're tempted to think, *Of course God can't make excuses, because it is God. Duh!* I would gently remind you to ask yourself, "Where did I come from?"

In other words, we all have potential that is far beyond our current mindset. This means we see ourselves as mere mortals riddled with flaws and imperfections. Yes, we human beings do make mistakes, and, yes, we do have our imperfections. However, we inevitably start making excuses when we focus exclusively on the limited and mortal part of our nature and forget about our true nature: our Source or our divine nature, the part of us that never dies.

We can reach our goals, ambitions, and desires when we remember that we came from a place of zero excuses. When we live true to our original nature and ditch our deceived self, we become powerful beings who are limited only by the conditioning that we allow to take hold in our minds.

Let's make sense of this by putting it into practical terms. I'm now going to contrast some of the aforementioned excuses that stem from our Deceived Self with the concurrent response from our Higher Self.

Deceived Self: "I am limited."

Higher Self: "The desires of my heart are part of my original nature; therefore, I have every tool and resource to manifest these desires into my life."

Deceived Self: "I need to remain reasonable to the expectations that I have on myself."

Higher Self: "Any desire that betters my character, my body, or my spirit is worth pursuing and is, thus, reasonable."

Deceived Self: "My past is indicative of my future."

Higher Self: "My past, whether good or bad, is meant to teach me. All things have a meaning and purpose, and I choose to learn from my past so that I might strengthen my future. My so-called failures are only strengthening and fortifying my resolve to achieve what I am seeking."

Deceived Self: "I lack time."

Higher Self: "I can prioritize anything into my life that is important to me. I can make anything happen if I use my time wisely. Nothing is more important than my health and well-being."

Deceived Self: "I lack ability."

Higher Self: "I come from a Source that doesn't comprehend lack, and I'm part of that Source. I have the ability to refine any skill or define any habit that I see fit."

Deceived Self: "It is not the right time for me to act on my desires."

Higher Self: "I live only in the present, and there is no better time than the present. I will act on my desires the very minute they come into my heart."

Deceived Self: "I don't have enough external support from my family or friends."

Higher Self: "I possess passion, desire, and drive. These are the only ingredients I really need. I will attract the right people to help me succeed, regardless of my current external circumstances."

Deceived Self: "I lack drive/desire."

Higher Self: "I create desire and drive by walking fearlessly and aggressively toward my goal, even if it's difficult. Success begets success, and it is my birthright to succeed."

When we live true to our original nature and ditch our Deceived Self, we become powerful beings who are limited only by the conditioning that we allow to take hold in our minds.

Deceived Self: "It's just the way I am."

Higher Self: "'The way I am' is my Higher Self at its very essence. Because this is true, I am fully capable of becoming whatever I want to become. I can refine my good qualities and eliminate the bad ones based on the desires of my heart."

Deceived Self: "Goal setting and achieving goals is not meant for me, because I'm incapable of achieving them. I have tried time and time again, and I can never seem to reach them."

Higher Self: "Anything that stirs a passion in my heart is therefore worthy of my time, effort, and determination. Therefore I am capable of achieving anything that I put my mind to."

Deceived Self: "I am genetically limited."

Higher Self: "My mind is never limited, and my body is capable of helping me achieve the desires of my heart."

Deceived Self: "My life is too busy."

Higher Self: "I'm never too busy to make time for personal development. I make time for activities that help me grow physically, mentally, emotionally, and spiritually."

Deceived Self: "I am too stressed to improve myself."

Higher Self: "Taking care of myself physically, spiritually, mentally, and emotionally is a fundamental responsibility of mine that helps to balance the stress in my life."

"I Have Reasons, Not Excuses": Deciphering the Difference between Truth and Excuse Making

One of my favorite definitions of an excuse is "any rational, justifiable, or reasonable explanation of programmed behavior that is contrary to proactive behavior and personal development." Further definition points to anything that stands in the way of you and your goal. To make this personal in your own life, look at some of your favorite excuses, and make sure they are rational, justifiable, and reasonable. If your own resistance stands between you and the desires of your heart and prevents you from taking action, it's an excuse—period.

You may justify your excuses in this way: "What if there is a death in the family, and I can't start my exercise program on the day that I planned. Isn't that a justifiable excuse?" We could go on and on about excuses and whether they can put a divide between you and your goal. I get it. Legitimate reasons come up in your life that are not excuses. What I would have you consider is the spirit of excuse making.

In the spirit of excuse making, we can *always* find a reasonable, justifiable, or rational reason for not taking action toward our goal. A simple method to tell the difference is to look at your consistency. For example, if you do have a death in your family, you may very well be justified in putting off your exercise program for a brief period. But if you find yourself coming up with consistent reasons for not exercising after the tragic event, you can rest assured that you have entered the realm of excuse making.

I know that there can be a fine line here, but it all comes down to the predominant patterns in your life. If you find yourself consistently moving toward your vision or goals with very few interruptions along the way, you can be sure that you're being proactive and not making excuses. In this mind-set, you will deal with life as it happens and then get right back on track. If, however, you find yourself being inconsistent by taking one step forward and then two steps back, it points to a pattern of excuse making regardless of external circumstances.

Living as Your Limitless Self

Ready or not, here it comes—a big, fat reality check! If you agree that you come from the Source of creation, love, and capability, does it stand to reason that you also have those abilities? Recall that your Source does not make excuses and functions and operates only in a state of faith and certitude.

Remember that your Higher Self is literally part of that source. As such, you also have limitless potential to create and manifest any goal that you set for yourself. Excuses are evidence that you have temporarily forgotten about your Higher Self and have resorted to believing the labels your ego has subconsciously manufactured for you.

My favorite definition of an excuse is this: "any rational, justifiable, or reasonable explanation of programmed behavior that is contrary to proactive behavior and personal development."

Let's bring this into a health and fitness context. Let's say, for example, that you want to lose one hundred pounds, and the desire of your heart is to go for it. Without properly conditioning your mind, you will likely invite your Deceived Self to run the show and flood your mind with a host of justifiable, reasonable, and rational reasons why it can't be done. Under these circumstances, you *choose* to limit yourself by ignoring what is your natural birthright: living as your Higher Self.

The Triple-A Solution

Now you're probably asking, "How do I live my life as my Higher Self?" The answer strikingly similar to the process of aligning the conditioning of your mind with the desires of your heart, as outlined in the Perception Reality Model in chapter 4. In fact, this is an integral part of the process and brings you into alignment with your Higher Self.

In addition, you can use a tool that I devised called the Triple-A Solution. Up to this point, I've written largely about the subconscious mind and how it controls human behavior. Ironically, the Triple-A Solution comes directly from the conscious faculty of your mind.

> Excuses are evidence that you have temporarily forgotten about
> your Higher Self and have resorted to believing the labels
> that your ego has subconsciously manufactured for you.

The Triple-A Solution uses the part of your brain that is responsible for 2 to 4 percent of your habitual behavior. This is in contrast to the subconscious part of your brain, which is responsible for 96 to 98 percent of all your habitual behavior, but is incapable of changing behavior. Remember—the only way to change an undesirable subconscious program and thereby change your behavior is through the use of your conscious mind. Ironic, isn't it? I chalk this up to God having a sense of humor.

Listed below are three A's from the Triple-A Solution. Keep in mind that you will need to use them repeatedly to combat your conditioned excuses. The more you use these techniques, the faster you'll free yourself from the bondage of excuse making.

A1: Awareness

We become steeped in excuse making because we have convinced ourselves that our excuses are valid, factual, and viable. Only through raising your awareness will you ever be capable of seeing excuses for what they truly are: excuses!

In the previous chapter, I discussed mind stories and the desires of your heart. The principle of awareness will allow you to identify both your conditioned beliefs and your excuses, which are often one and the same. Remember that negatively conditioned beliefs and excuses are nothing more than barricades standing between you and your goals.

If we fail to raise our level of awareness, we will always revert back to excuse making. For example, if you find yourself making statements such as, "Well, I get this whole excuse-making thing, but my excuse is my reality right now, so there is not much I can do about it," rest assured that your level of awareness needs to be elevated so you can advance to the A2 listed below.

Action Steps

The next time you find yourself entertaining an excuse, stop yourself immediately and become aware of its presence. For example, if you're having the thought, I *don't have time to exercise today*, raise your level of awareness by quarantining that thought and saying to yourself, *I just made an excuse! Interesting how my conditioned mind is trying to stop me from achieving my goal.*

As silly as this sounds, I promise you that your increased awareness will take your consciousness to a new level. I invite you to think about what you're doing here. You're directly challenging the conditioning of your mind and calling it out. This is where the boxing gloves start to come off. The fight has now begun, and you are ready for the second A.

A2: Acceptance

Banishing excuses can be difficult because they're located in your subconscious mind. When you try to challenge an existing excuse, a part of your brain called the psychocybernetic mechanism kicks into high gear. This mechanism is similar to a thermostat set at sixty-five degrees in the dead of winter. Although the temperature outside is much cooler, the thermostat is responsible for keeping the inside air at sixty-five degrees.

In like manner, when you challenge an existing belief, you often find that your psychocybernetic mechanism goes into a defensive mode to try to maintain the status quo. Physiologically, your limbic system can secrete hormones, such as adrenaline and cortisol, that make you feel as though something is wrong. This primal response is hardwired into the human nervous system and is meant to protect you from harm.

In prehistoric times, this came in handy in helping humans remember paths and how to avoid saber-toothed tigers. In modern times, it can help you in many ways, but it can concomitantly confuse you as you seek to make changes. The secret is to recognize when this part of your brain has been falsely activated. As you seek to make changes, this mechanism will cause you temporary discomfort, and that's okay. It's trying to help you stay "safe," so it's doing its job. Recognize it for what it is, appreciate it, and then move forward with your goals, despite its false warnings.

Action Step

The key here is to combine the power of step 1 (awareness) with acceptance. Once you become aware of the excuse you're making ("I don't have time"), you can own that excuse by stating the following: "I just made the excuse that I don't have time. I now claim this excuse as mine, and I own it."

Essentially, you're raising your hand and saying, "Yep! That was my excuse." This is the antithesis of denial or getting angry or resentful when confronted with your excuses. Now that you're aware of your excuse and have accepted it as yours, it's time to tangle with the game-changing power of the third A.

A3: Action!

This is where the rubber meets the road! It's also the hardest A of the Triple-A Solution. I can't tell you how many times I've completed the first two steps and then been stumped by this one. Because we are stuck in habitual thinking patterns and ways of living, it can be difficult to take action on our newly formed vision and goals. It's analogous to getting out of our warm beds on a cold winter morning. We don't want to move!

Although it will be hard at first, you don't have to tackle it all at once. The very act of completing the first two A's will have taken you a very long way already. If you have made it to this point, you're ready for the next action step.

Action Step

The next time you become aware of your excuses and own them, do the *opposite* of what your excuse is calling for. In other words, take the action that is the opposite of your excuse. For example, the next time you make the excuse of not having time, you do two very distinct but equally important things:

1. *Mentally* and verbally state the opposite. For example, say to yourself, *I will make the time for the desire of my heart because nothing can keep me from achieving it.*
2. *Physically* plan it into your schedule, and do it. If the desire of your heart is to lose twenty-five pounds, and you know you should exercise, write it into your schedule and physically do it.

You may have to rearrange or omit less important things in your daily schedule to make time for this, but that's okay because it's worth it. If you find this process painful, just realize that you're pouring fresh concrete over well-worn pathways in your brain. The pain of your psychocybernetic mechanism will fade over time, and you'll find pleasure in your new way of thinking. I promise!

It's time to go deeper and extract the most stubborn and insidious excuses of them all.

CHAPTER 6

THEMES AND MEMES

Shedding Light on Your Darkest and Most "Damming" Excuses

Don't blame society. *You are* the society!
—Meme Quotes

It's a little embarrassing to admit, but I've never been close to my extended family. If my cousin walked right by me today, I wouldn't know him. However, I do have some memories of family gatherings when I was a small boy. In particular, I remember a small series of family reunions that will forever be etched into memory with crystal-clear detail.

Specifically, I can never forget our Thanksgivings between 1986 and 1988, mainly because of my uncle Chris, whose name has been changed to protect the guilty. He was a massive individual with audible clout to go along with it.

I remember Chris's comments during dinner as though it were yesterday. Sitting back on his chair, he bellowed, "Once you're past the age of thirty-five, your metabolism hits the dust." Laughter and nods followed. He went on: "Ever since my football injury in high school, I haven't had the function in my knee that I would like. The doctor tells me that I should exercise, but I would like to see him exercise with my bum knee!" Uncle Chris was a truck driver, which played right into his next comment: "My work keeps me seated all day long, and I don't have a set schedule, so I can't exercise."

The monologue went on for at least fifteen minutes as more excuses spewed from Uncle Chris's mouth. I was only eight years old during this initial conversation. The next year I returned, and nothing had changed with Uncle Chris except his weight. He must have been 330 pounds with no sign of changing. "I'm just too old and worn out," was one of his favorites, along with "Life's a bitch, and then you die."

Even at the ripe old age of eight, I was in a trancelike state as I observed my Uncle Chris. Here was a man who hardly worked because of frequent sickness and was slowly losing his family; his wife worked to pick up his slack. Knowing deep within his soul that he was killing himself with his lifestyle habits, he lived in a constant state of denial by grasping for cultural themes that seemed to justify his actions.

All Uncle Chris's statements are far more than trite clichés in our society. They are a subset of conditioning that I call themes and memes.

Themes

Recall our discussion in chapter 4 about the Perceived Reality Model and the power of conditioning. We discussed that conditioned beliefs control both our desirable and our undesirable lifestyle habits. With this concept in mind, it will be easy for you to understand the concept of a cultural or personal *theme*.

> Themes can be good or bad or anywhere in between.
> Ultimately, they have a profound influence on the way
> we behave both individually and collectively.

A theme is a collective conditioned belief that stems from cultural norms, religious training, societal expectations, parental expectations, and the like. Themes are usually taken for granted and are rarely challenged by the average person. Most of the time, they're considered normal and advantageous to society. Take, for example, the following cultural themes that are common in America today:

- "Once you're in high school, you need to start thinking long and hard about what you want to do with your life."
- "It's important to consider career options and interests once you get into high school."
- "Eat more veggies."
- "Adequate sleep is important."
- "Society demands the raising of responsible and hard-working children to ensure the successful future of the human race."
- "Attending church on Sunday makes you a good Christian."
- "Justice, liberty, and fairness are principles of the American way of life."

The list could go on almost infinitely. Although themes are rarely challenged and often thought of as good, they are neutral. They can be good or bad or anywhere in between. Ultimately, they have a profound influence on the way we carry out our lives and behave both individually and collectively.

Imagine you're at a baseball game and "The Star-Spangled Banner" begins to play. You immediately put your hand over your heart because, as a society, we have a theme that dictates that you "show respect for your country." I believe this to be a good theme.

Now let's switch gears and talk about the cousin of the theme: the meme. Although closely related, memes carry the potential of crippling society and stunting your individual progress.

Memes: Closing Your Mind and Damming Your Progress

Let's go a little bit deeper and find out where these culture themes originate. *Virus of the Mind,* a best-selling book by Richard Brodie, is filled with intriguing content that will change the way you perceive your world. It discusses the idea of a meme. Quite fittingly, the word sounds like *gene.* I've heard many definitions of a meme, but the one I prefer is this: "A thought, attitude, or belief that subtly or aggressively influences human behavior."

Characteristics of Memes

You may want to study these common characteristics so you can identify and destroy negative memes in your own life.

Memes Are the Basic Unit of Cultural Thought Transmission

Think of a meme as a type of gene—the basic unit of human DNA that carries information that's spread from the mother and father to their offspring. In like fashion, a meme is the basic unit of cultural transmission. I frequently host college-age interns in my coaching center, and I often hear them use the expression "That's sick!" That statement perplexed me until I realized it was pertaining to something cool, awesome, and thrilling.

This example illustrates how a meme works. The word *sick* usually carries with it negative connotations. We have given this particular word distinction, and therefore have drawn certain conclusions given its meaning. Whether we know it or not, we feel and act a certain way when we hear somebody uses *sick*. When teenagers got their hands on it, they rememed it. We repackage something according to our own likes and dictates. This can be done personally and collectively as a society.

Allow me to draw you a fictitious scenario of how this particular meme may have originated. Imagine a group of teenage boys hanging out at a monster truck show. A truck tears up the ramp, gets at least thirty feet of air, and crashes on its side after rolling three times. One of the teenagers stands up in the bleachers and yells for the first time, "That was sick, bro!" His friends roll in laughter at the absurdity of his statement, yet they can't get over the coolness of his newly coined phrase.

Trying to get in on the action of the new phrase, another teenage boy spots an attractive girl in a miniskirt and yells to his buddies, "Man, she's sick!"

Instantly, a meme is created and is ready to spread like wildfire to every teenager in America.

Memes Spread and Replicate Depending on Their Societal Impact

In the story above, *sick* was instantly popular. It resonated as a viable unit of information in the teenagers' heads, and thus it continued to spread from mouth to mouth and, more importantly, from mind to mind. This is exactly how memes work. An idea, thought, or attitude is introduced into the mind of one person, and it immediately begins to spread and replicate to other minds like a virus.

> If a meme is unpopular and has no perceived
> value, it will eventually fade and die out.

The strength of a meme is contingent on its popularity and its perceived value. The "sick" meme is obviously popular because we hear people everywhere use it under many different circumstances. It also gives those who use it perceived value. This value comes from feeling cool and "in" when they use the phrase. Every teenager wants to become part of the cool crowd that uses an "in" dialect. It bolsters ego, provides a false sense of self, and keeps friends close by. This all adds up to a tremendous amount of value. If a meme is unpopular and has no perceived value, it will eventually fade and die out.

> The strength of a meme is contingent on its
> popularity and its perceived value.

A good example of this can be seen in the food industry. As a teenager, I remember at least two new Snickers bars that appeared on the scene. Initially, everybody got caught up in the marketing hype, and consumers began buying them and liking them. Unfortunately for Snickers, their marketing memes weren't popular enough to make the long-term splash they were hoping for.

Fashion designers, movie makers, and pop-culture pimps are always trying to introduce memes that become popular and influential. A popular tagline or slogan for a business is a meme that can mean either millions or mediocrity.

Memes Are Neutral

A meme is a thought, a belief, or an attitude that can subtly or aggressively influence behavior, both individually and culturally. This form of mental conditioning can be either good or bad. An example of a negative meme would be not exercising based on a conditioned belief: "I have bad genes, so why should I exercise?" I've heard this meme numerous times as a personal trainer, and it illustrates how negative memes can profoundly influence behavior.

On the other end of the spectrum, nobody would argue a meme that states, "Education is a good thing," is a bad meme. It's a form of conditioning that is helpful to society, and most would agree that its proliferation is advantageous to all. *The point here is to program your mind with positive memes and eliminate the negative ones.*

Memes Are Stored Subconsciously and Acted on Subconsciously

Earlier I mentioned that all habits are stored subconsciously. To reiterate, 96 to 98 percent of all human behavior stems from the subconscious mind. For example, if you believe you lack self-control because your parents lacked self-control, the problem is not in your genes; it's in your memes.

I've heard these and other memes many times in my career, and to be truthful, I always find myself saddened and somewhat defensive. I'm saddened because I know that people uttering the memes are only replaying a subconscious program that they aren't even aware of. I'm defensive because I see divine beings that are capable of anything and are unaware of their inner greatness because they are beholden to their internal memes.

> If you believe that you have low self-control because
> your parents had low self-control, the problem
> is not in your genes; it's in your memes.

Memes Are Perceived as Reality

Any form of conditioning that's reinforced over and over becomes reality in our minds, even if it isn't reality in actuality. Think long and hard about that last statement because it applies to the memes that we've been subjected to and victimized with. In other words, we believe our memes to be reality once they are cemented into our subconscious.

With no intention of judgment or insensitivity, let's use an example of a woman who has been abused by more than one man. It's likely that she perceives all men as harmful and selfish, although this is not the case. If this meme continues to rule her subconscious, she will lead a life of solitude, bitterness, and resentment toward all men and toward life in general. The same can be said of men facing similar situations with women.

Memes become our reality when we don't challenge their validity or ask the vital question "Is that really true?" In fact, we become possessive of memes because we view them as truth. This can breed rigidity, stubbornness, and an unwillingness to change if those memes are left unchallenged through reasonable questioning.

Two of my uncle Chris's favorite memes—and therefore his reality—were "fatness comes with oldness" and "life is a bitch, and then you die." These and a hundred other memes justified his gluttonous behavior and created a reality for him that nobody would desire. By rehearsing these cultural memes, which he had absorbed during the course of his lifetime, he locked himself into his own perceived reality. By so doing, he was subconsciously trying to protect himself from the consequences of his own behavior.

> Memes become our reality when we don't challenge their
> validity or ask the vital question "Is that really true?"

Memes Require Conscious Rejection to Uproot and Change Habits

Let's quickly review the ultimate irony of mental reconditioning. We know that our subconscious mind is responsible for 96 to 98 percent of our habitual behavior. This leaves our conscious mind with a whopping 2 to 4 percent control over our behavior. So what am I telling you? That your everyday behaviors are governed by your subconscious mind. If you aren't pleased with your current reality, you must change your subconscious mind with your conscious mind. In other words, the 2 to 4 percent must trump the 96 to 98 percent. Ironic, huh?

The solution for reprogramming your mind comes back to the principle of awareness. Although your conscious mind has little power over your habits, it does have the ability to recognize the habits and behaviors that you would like to change. In other words, you *do* have the ability to observe your behavior and select what is unacceptable to you. From there, you can consciously make a decision to change it. This requires you to raise your awareness drastically at the conscious level.

The principle of awareness dictates that you become keenly conscious of the thoughts and behaviors that are destructive to your vision and goals. Let's say, for example, that you've formed a habit of eating brownies and ice cream when you sit down and relax for the evening. Let's assume that you've indulged this habit for twenty-five years and justified it with a plethora of memes. At this point, your behavior is subconscious, which means you don't question it, challenge it, or even think about it.

> You do have the ability to observe your behavior and
> select what is unacceptable to you. From there you
> can consciously make a decision to change it.

If you then set a goal to eat less ice cream and brownies, you have become aware of your behavior. The challenging part comes when the moment presents itself to you, and you're forced to elevate your awareness or consciousness yet again. When you come home and get into your routine, you need to be aware of your old behavioral pattern so that you can *consciously* replace it with something healthier. The trick is to repeat this pattern multiple times until the old pattern is replaced and the meme is destroyed.

Memes Are Often Linked with Excuse Making

All memes are not excuses, but all excuses are memes. Let that one digest for a minute. Memes are nothing more than conditioned beliefs that limit you from taking action toward your inner desires. If you stack this up to the Perceived Reality Model, you'll find that this fits nicely into stages 2 to 4 of the model.

This might be hard for you to believe because your memes have become your reality. Let's say that you have been using the time meme ("I don't have time") to excuse yourself from exercise and proper nutrition. If you have harbored this meme over an extended period, you will surely view it as reality. This is how my Perception Reality Model received its name.

So, to substantiate my point, let's follow the meme/excuse fact trail and see where it takes us:

1. A meme is a thought, attitude, or belief that subtly or aggressively influences individual or cultural behavior.
2. We all harbor memes, both good and bad.
3. All memes are not excuses, but all excuses are memes.
4. Excuses limit our actions toward obtaining the desires of our hearts.
5. Because memes are a form of mental conditioning that we *perceive as reality*, they bring us a false sense of security regarding our limiting behaviors.
6. We continue in our limiting behavior, which then activates our conscious mind and makes us feel guilt or that we need to correct our actions.
7. We view the corrective action as difficult.
8. We make more excuses to justify our behaviors and reinforce our memes because they are the path of least resistance.

Take heart because you're learning how to unravel this self-replicating process in your life and to take responsibility for everything that happens in your life. When you do this, you truly become empowered to take your life in any direction you desire.

All memes are not excuses, but all excuses are memes.

Memes Have the Power to Dictate Behavior

The bottom line is this: memes and excuses dictate the behavior that you want eliminate. This is the ultimate paradox. Why? On one hand, you want to rid yourself of behaviors that keep you from obtaining the desire of your heart, right? On the other hand, you continue to energize beliefs that have morphed into memes and excuses.

My uncle Chris desired to change his behavior but was subservient to the dominant memes stored in his subconscious mind. These memes came out in full display as excuse making. His excuses were his conscious interpretation of his subconscious programming.

At this point, you may be saying to yourself, *Well, that really sucks! Based on what I just read, it looks like I'm screwed and will be subservient to my memes and excuses for the rest of my life because they are coming from my subconscious mind.* Nothing could be further from the truth. You now possess the element of *awareness,* which serves as your starting point to free you from your themes, memes, and excuses.

Congratulations, you now possess knowledge that less than 1 percent of the population has. Let's hop to the next chapter, where you'll take this knowledge and turn it into action.

CHAPTER 7

GENES AND MEMES

The Size of Your Genes Does Not Determine the Size of Your Jeans

I have bred, nurtured, and earned my virtues;
they are mine. As for my vices, they belong to my parents.
—Griff Neilson

Her name was Leslie (name changed), and she stood at five five and weighed nearly 230 pounds. She was a sweet-hearted woman who was my client when I was a young twenty-six-year-old personal trainer. I quickly became friends with Leslie as we started on our mutual mission to improve her health and fitness.

As a personal trainer, I was accustomed to hearing all sorts of juicy excuses from my clients as to why they ate junk food or why they didn't exercise. Leslie's type of excuse making was different. She blamed just about everything on her genetics.

Depression, laziness, a proclivity toward alcohol, anger, and jealously were just a few of the things she happily blamed on her genes. I could have sworn that she had scientifically isolated each and every one of her genes that were responsible for her shortcomings. It was as if she were saying, "This is my anger gene, and over here is my overeating gene, and here is my excuse-making gene!"

At the time, I was skeptical about her genetic arguments, but I didn't have any ammunition against her relentless barrage. She always couched her excuses with the insinuation that she couldn't possibly do anything about it. She truly displayed a victim mentality, which frustrated me, partially because I didn't have the professional resources to deal with her.

As the weeks passed, I began to notice a pattern. When Leslie was on a roll with her exercise and nutrition, her body fat seemed to melt off as she desired, and she was generally happy. When she let life get in the way of her efforts, she invariably fell off the wagon, and the genetic excuses returned with a vengeance. In her own words, she instantly became "fat, lazy, and unmotivated" because that was just who she was—or so she claimed.

My Disclaimer

I'm aware that the topic of genetics can be a touchy one. It seems to be one of those taboo subjects that we're scared to talk about because it's politically incorrect to suggest that anyone might be to blame for his or her attitudes, personalities, health, fitness, and nutritional habits. Yet, is it so audacious to suggest that genes might have some influence over these areas?

My disclaimer here is that I'm being insensitive in any way. Rather, I want to share with you some of the new science that suggests we have more control over our health than we give ourselves credit for. In particular, I'd like to speak about your genes versus the environment that you provide to each and every one of your millions of cells. In essence, we're going to talk about nature versus nurture and how it pertains to your mental and physical health.

My Genetically Modified View

I wish I had coached Leslie a little later in my holistic coaching career. As my career progressed, my knowledge and understanding of genetic influence versus environmental influence changed dramatically after reading *The Biology of Belief* by Dr. Bruce Lipton. In the past, I was confused when clients blamed their lack of progress on their genes because I didn't understand that we have the power to change our lives and our bodies through the thoughts we think and the food we consume.

I am in no way qualified to delve into the hard science that Lipton so eloquently elaborates in his book, so I highly recommend reading his book cover to cover. For the scope of this book, I'll touch on some of the most important points from Lipton's masterpiece and discuss how they can help you to exorcise your excuses.

Here's a sample: "I came to the conclusion that we are not victims of our genes, but masters of our fates, able to create lives overflowing with peace, happiness, and love."

Bam! Wow! Shebang! What did he just say? Is he telling us that our genes are not the end-all and be-all? Is he saying what I think he's saying? Yes! This is exactly what he's saying, and the science that proves it is fascinating, to say the least.

In essence, Lipton discusses the principle of interdependence as it relates to the millions of cells in the human organism. Each cell works with countless others to keep the organism as a whole alive. He further states that *the environment* that our cells live in encourages certain genes to express themselves, while others are left suppressed. In other words, our physiological environment turns genes on or off. For example, if you provide your cells with a garbage environment by eating garbage food, you should not be surprised when you get a disease, such as cancer.

At this point, you may be shouting at the pages of this book, asking, "So, you're telling me that my genetics have no role in the extra layer of fat around my midsection?" I can't answer as Lipton would, but from what I've learned, we are the ones who create the environment that our cells live in. To reiterate, this environment is responsible for allowing certain genes to express themselves or not. In the case of fat storage, certain genes will be expressed or suppressed, depending on the right environment.

Consider the old cliché "You are what you eat." This statement is not metaphorical in any sense of the word. We literally become what we eat at the molecular level, and these same molecules make your physical body.

With this in mind, is it outrageous to suggest that we have the power to control our health and fitness? Do we have the power to suppress certain diseases, such as type 2 diabetes, high blood pressure, coronary artery disease, and even cancer? The research unequivocally states that we do. For example, scientists have proven that excessive amounts of sugar drastically increase our likelihood of contracting type 2 diabetes or a metabolic syndrome by increasing the chances of being overweight and obese.

I, of course, acknowledge that certain diseases can be traced to genetics. Dr. Lipton has said on this subject,

> There is no doubt that some diseases, like Huntington's chorea, beta thalassemia, and cystic fibrosis can be blamed entirely on one faulty gene. But single-gene disorders affect less than two percent of the population; the vast majority of people come into this world with genes that should enable them to live a happy and healthy life. The diseases that are today's scourges—diabetes, heart disease, and cancer—short circuit a happy and healthy life. These diseases, however, are not the result of a single gene but of complex interactions among multiple genes and environmental factors.[1]

If, like Leslie, we believe that our genetics are to blame for our physical makeup, our mental fortitude and ability, our personality, our money-earning capacity, our attitude, and our overall health, we give ourselves a perfect excuse not to act on the desires of our heart. After all, we can't control our genes, because they control us, right?

---

[1] Bruce Lipton, PhD, *The Biology of Belief* (Alexandria, NSW: Hay House, 2005), 20–21.

Let's say that you want to lose weight, but you simultaneously foster a programmed meme that says, "I want to lose weight, but it is so much harder for me than anybody else because of my genetics." With this meme running in the background of your mind, you will be hard-pressed to take action because you're convinced that you're already screwed-over. Can you now see how genes and memes are related?

Science is telling us that the DNA double helix is not the sole determining factor of our health and fitness. As mentioned previously, a select few genes can have devastating effects on our health, and they should be respected. But the fascinating field of biology called epigenetics is begging to be explored, contemplated, and further researched. Lipton goes on to explain this intriguing and ever-expanding field of research:

> The science of epigenetics, which literally means "control above genetics," profoundly changes our understanding of how life is controlled (Pray 2004; Silverman 2004). In the last decade, epigenetic research has established that DNA blueprints passed down through genes are not set in concrete at birth. Genes are not destiny! Environmental influences, including nutrition, stress, and emotions can modify those genes without changing their basic blueprint. And those modifications, epigeneticists have discovered, can be passed on to future generations as surely as DNA blueprints are passed on via the double helix (Reik and Walter 2001, Surani 2001).[2]

While this information challenges existing beliefs and old-school science, it seems to make sense. Think of it this way: Why would I be put here by my creative Source and then told that I have no control over my health, my well-being, and my life in general? Then the question each of us must ask is this: "If my nutritional status, my mental health, and my physical health is, indeed, hardwired and preprogrammed by my genetics, why am I equipped to make every one of these areas better?"

---

[2] Ibid., p. 37.

Is it not common sense that we can enhance the environment of our cells by eating whole, natural foods? Does it not further make sense that if I provide the right environment for my cells, they will provide the right environment for my entire body, which is a collection of cells?

> Each of us must ask, "If my nutritional status, my mental health, and my physical health is, indeed, hardwired and preprogrammed by my genetics, why am I equipped as a human being to make every one of these areas better?"

This then begs the question "What can I do to ensure that I'm providing the right environment for my cells to thrive so that I can preserve my health and function optimally?" I'll cover this question extensively in chapters 12 and 13, but for now I'm going to tackle the two big ones. If you can tackle these two big ones, they will trickle into just about every other area of your life.

Providing the Right Nutritional Environment

To back up the claims of Lipton and other scientists, consider what the World Health Organization has stated on it website about the preventability of cancer: "At least one-third of all cancer cases are preventable. Prevention offers the most cost-effective long-term strategy for the control of cancer."[3]

Other highly respectable organizations have stated that up to 70 percent of cancers are preventable through healthy nutritional practices. Every time I announce this statistic in a public-speaking setting, audience members have shocked looks on their faces.

Think about it: If we are what we eat (and this is true beyond any argument), why should it surprise us that eating unnatural substances like artificial sweeteners, sugar, colors, and dyes harms our health and increases our chances for contracting cancer and other diseases?

---

[3]   World Health Organization, "Cancer prevention," April 4, 2016, http://www.who.int/cancer/prevention/en/.

This book is dedicated to helping you recondition your mind so you can consciously move toward the healthy lifestyle that you deserve. I'm including nutrition here because it directly influences thinking patterns. This happens from multiple angles.

To use a simple example, consider what happens in your body when you chronically eat processed, nutrient-depleted food. First, it raises your insulin to unhealthy levels, and when your blood sugar inevitably crashes, you're introduced to counter-regulatory hormones that do not make you feel good. In fact, they make you feel sluggish and weak, and they take away your clarity, focus, and sense of well-being.

In this physical state, it's difficult, if not impossible, to have positive thoughts and feelings. Most Americans are so accustomed to eating unhealthy food that they become complacent and even unaware that they're living at a suboptimal level of health and vitality. This state of mind can be mistaken as normal. And a low level of physical and mental awareness makes it easy to neglect a healthy lifestyle.

In summary, when you eat like crap, you feel like crap. When you feel like crap, you think like crap. When you think like crap, your life becomes crap, and you're left to wonder how you got caught in this vicious cycle in the first place.

The nutritional solution is simple. Eat whole, natural foods, which you were designed to eat. If you need to first obtain a PhD in chemistry to pronounce the items on a food label, it's probably not a good idea to eat that food. It's not the intention of this book to delve into proper nutritional practices, but if you remember to use common sense and make fruits and veggies the foundation of your diet, you'll go far in preventing a negative environment for the countless millions of cells that comprise your body. In chapter 13, we'll go deeper into this subject.

Providing the Right Mental Environment

Two paragraphs ago, I told you that when you feel like crap, you think like crap. This is where the chicken and the egg question comes into play. Which one comes first: eating like crap, which spurs a negative physiological state, which then makes you feel like crap, *or* thinking like crap, which spurs a crappy physiological state that makes you want to eat like crap?

> When you eat like crap, you feel like crap. When you feel like crap, you think like crap. When you think like crap, your life becomes crap, and you're left to wonder how you ever got caught in this vicious cycle in the first place.

The answer to this riddle is *both.* Negative forms of thinking and nutrition will lead you to a negative physiological state. This is the conundrum that must be avoided at all costs. If you intend to control your health, it becomes necessary to control the following:

- thoughts, feelings, and emotions
- what goes into your mouth

According to epigenetic research, *we* are the ones who ultimately determine the expression of our gene pool. We influence the expression of our genes based on the mental and physical environment that we place ourselves in day in and day out.

Bridging the Gap between Your Mind and Your Body

As we discussed earlier, your subconscious mind is responsible for 96 to 98 percent of all your behaviors. This is why the little things, such as the toilet paper being "hung wrong" in the bathroom, get on your nerves. Think of it: You've been taught from the time you were young that the toilet paper is to be hung a certain way—the *right way.* This right way was logged into your subconscious mind, and you've been running this belief system as a truth. If that truth is violated in your inner world, there is hell to pay, both for you, because you become irritated, and for others, because of your self-righteous corrective behavior.

Now let's look at how this silly little toilet paper example can affect your internal physiology. To do this, I need to remind you that everything in this universe is comprised of energy, and thought is no exception. Thought is an intangible form of energy that vibrates at different frequencies. Thoughts are analogous to a radio station in that each vibrates at its own unique frequency.

Positive thoughts tend to vibrate at a faster frequency than negative ones. These frequencies have very specific influences on our cells. For example, thought energy can activate or inhibit cell activity depending on the vibrational frequency of the thought energy.

Let's say that you have a pessimistic nature, and you always see the glass half empty. With this mind-set, your brain is always producing thought patterns of a lower vibratory intensity. As a walking mass of intelligently organized energy, your body constantly intakes and transmits energy. To put it a different way, your energy is never lost, merely transformed. So, if you're always harboring negative thoughts, feelings, and emotions, you're literally setting your body up for dis-ease. "How?" you might ask.

Let me make this very simple. Imagine a top-of-the-line sports car designed to run on premium fuel with a high octane rating. In essence, this car needs a high-grade fuel so it can perform at a very high level. A low-grade fuel in the engine can bog the engine down, create sludge in the cylinders, and create oxidation that will stress the engine and chip away at the car's innate potential.

Likewise, your body is "tuned" to vibrate at a certain intensity, which then creates a unique energy frequency. This frequency can be thought of as your sweet spot. When you hit your sweet spot, you experience health and well-being. When you're vibrating at this frequency, you naturally and effortlessly feel good, think good, and perform well.

The fuel that you choose to give your body through both physiological factors (nutrition and lifestyle) and psychological factors (thought patterns and habits) determines your rate of energy vibration. This rate of vibration dictates your energy, functionality, and vitality. If you fuel yourself with the right thoughts, food, and exercise, your body will be able to *resonate* at your sweet spot. Resonating at an ideal frequency will help you live a positive and exciting life.

To put this into practical terms, let's consider two extremes. For our first example, we'll look at a case study of a man we'll call Bill. After waking up each morning, Bill routinely begins his day with a parade of negative thoughts, such as "Why does my back hurt?" and "Man, I have a bunch of things that I don't want to do today." Day in and day out, he rethinks these and other negative thoughts. Keep in mind that Bill's thoughts are nothing more than energy patterns that carry with them a certain frequency of vibration. His thought patterns are low and slow.

Nutritionally, Bill chooses to eat processed and sugary foods that aren't conducive to his health. So he faces a double whammy. He is already in the habit of filling his mind with low-energy thought frequencies, and he compounds his problem with low-quality food. This takes a tremendous physiological toll on Bill's body. In essence, he has placed his body into a state of stress without possessing sufficient physiological resources to buffer it.

Bill's energetic state now begins to integrate with his cell proteins, so his cells are forced to express themselves below their genetic potential. This could have easily been remedied with higher frequency, positive thoughts. To make matters worse, Bill's poor diet forced his cells to process high acid levels from a high-sugar diet. As a result, his body began to vibrate at a level far below his sweet spot, or homeostasis. He now becomes a perfect candidate for the following mental states, ailments, and diseases:

- low energy or lethargy
- irritability
- sugar dependency
- forgetfulness
- brain fog and inability to concentrate

- metabolic disorders such as insulin resistance or type 2 diabetes
- cardiovascular disease
- a gloom and doom perspective
- moodiness
- fungal and parasite infections
- hypochondriac behaviors
- reactive behavior
- addictions
- many more diseases, both acute and chronic

When you understand your body to be a physical unit of intelligently channeled energy, it makes sense that it becomes highly sensitive and susceptible to self-induced and destructive energy patterns. The acceptance of this logic requires an open mind, diligent research, and personal experience. When you accept that good health stems from appropriate energy management, the equation of good health becomes simple and easy to implement.

In the West, we have a hard time with holistic thinking. We struggle with the idea that the human body is an interdependent "system of systems." Instead, we love to compartmentalize everything, and we get stuck in a "this for that" mentality. When something goes wrong with our body, we go to doctors, and they say, "Oh, your head hurts? Take this pill. Your stomach is upset? Have this antacid."

Rarely do we have the courage to realize that *we* have an enormous role in promoting our own health. We are not merely victims of our genes. I'm not saying that genes can't play a part—they certainly can and do. Nobody is disputing that. However, the vast majority of people blame their diseases, ailments, and lack of success on their genes and forget that they play a tremendous role in their health.

When you understand your body to be a physical unit
of intelligently channeled energy, it makes sense that
it becomes highly sensitive and susceptible to self-
induced and highly destructive energy patterns.

The sad reality is that we tend to excuse away our health, falsely believing that we have little or no control over our health destiny. But we are powerful beyond our limited perceptions, and we have far more ability to shape our physiological and psychological destinies than we give ourselves credit for.

Now let's look at the other end of the spectrum with the second case study. "John" came to me with an arsenal of excuses, a morbid case of obesity, and prediabetes to boot. His proclivity to make excuses was off the charts, and he was loaded with one sob story after another as to why he wasn't able to take any action on the instructions I gave him.

During a particularly difficult coaching session, John was challenging everything I said, and I decided to act on an inspiration. Not being an aggressive person by nature, I decided to shock John. I stood up out of my chair, raised my voice to a very high level, and said, "John, why the hell are you here? You're wasting your money and your time by challenging everything I say. If you know all the answers, I suggest you pick your ass out of that chair and get the hell out of my office so you can start your own holistic coaching practice. If you don't know all the answers, and you're sitting here for a reason, I would appreciate it if you shut your mouth for a measly five minutes and do exactly what I tell you to do."

I could not believe what I had just said. Yikes! If any professional life coach had seen my antics, he or she would have cringed and feared for my career. However, John and I had formed a strong working relationship that convinced him to heed my advice; he knew I cared for him and loved him. I then took him through some of the techniques that you are now learning in this book.

Initially, John was still a little resistant to my coaching, but sensing my bullheaded determination, he didn't challenge me. I took him through the process of stating positive affirmations, declarations, and incantations. I had him yell them with emotion and with a smile on his face. This was hard for John because he was used to scowling. At the end of our extended two-hour session, he left with a singed document stating that he would do the same routine for three weeks straight.

> When you accept that good health stems from
> appropriate energy management, the equation of good
> health becomes simple and easy to implement.

At the conclusion of those three weeks, John sat in my office as he had done multiple times. He wasn't frowning nor was he radiating his usual negative energy. This time, John was smiling ear to ear, and he proceeded to give me a slight nod of approval. I was immediately relieved. He then pulled out his homework and began to tell me about his journey during the previous three weeks.

In short, John had retrained himself in the ways he spoke, walked, ate, and thought. It was as if he'd gone to a three-week boot camp for his brain. In those life-changing three weeks, he became *aware* of his negative thoughts and self-limiting internal dialogues. He became aware of the junk foods he was consuming. He became aware of how they affected his mind and his body.

In other words, he became aware of his self-created negative energy and how it was ruling his life in every area. Through continuing to implement the concepts that you are now learning, John lost over seventy pounds, cut his sugar intake to less than forty grams per day, and began exercising six days per week. His life was changed forever.

To this day, John is one of the happiest people I know. Sure he has bad days like the rest of us, but he now refuses to make excuses and allow negative energy into his life for extended periods. People have subsequently called me and asked, "What did you do to so radically change John?" I'm always more than happy to share our unconventional story.

So, what happened to John? He took control of his physiology and his psychology. By so doing, he allowed every cell of his body to be penetrated with a high-vibrating energy that brought health rather than disease. In essence, he *returned* to his natural state of being.

Through his consciousness, he was able to override deeply embedded subconscious programs that had ruled his behavior for decades. By allowing positive energy to penetrate each and every one of his cells, he allowed them to express themselves according to their innate potential. It was as though a weight had been lifted off his naturally resilient body and mind.

Although I can't physiologically prove what went on in John's body, I experienced firsthand the power of positive intention and consciousness. In the following chapters, I'll explore with you the methods that changed his life. My hope is that you will take the following principles and allow them to change your life as well.

CHAPTER 8

PUTTING YOUR EXCUSES
ON THE BULL'S-EYE

Creating Your Dream through the Power of Focus

Concentrate all of your thoughts upon the work at hand.
The sun's rays do not burn until brought to a focus.
—Alexander Graham Bell

Personal development coach Tony Robbins has frequently stated, "Where focus goes, energy flows." The power of this statement can be understood only by applying the seemingly mystical power of focus. I know from experience. In late 2015, I became certified as a level 3 CHEK Holistic Lifestyle coach, which has been one of the most enriching experiences of my life. Many of the concepts and principles that I'm teaching you in this book have roots in my holistic training.

As part of our training, we coaches were advised to participate in a dietary antifungal and parasitic cleanse. Now, if you're thinking, *Yeah, I have been on a cleanse, and they are pretty cool,* let me assure you that this particular type of cleansing is not as sexy as you might think. It calls for the elimination of all sugar, including natural sources, such as fruit, starchy veggies, legumes, lentils, grains, dairy, gluten, and a host of other foods common to our American diet—for six months! In addition, I had to follow a strict supplemental regimen that required a lot of time and money.

I have always prided myself in begin a clean eater, so I considered myself a perfect candidate for this cleanse. However, I was a little intimidated with all the restrictions and the structure involved. I was being asked to eliminate many of the healthy foods that comprised a large portion of my diet.

With these restrictions in mind, I participated in some fence sitting for about a month, going back and forth on whether to commit 100 percent to the cleanse. I also wavered because I enjoyed indulging in a weekly cheat meal—my time to relax and indulge in foods that I would otherwise avoid. I enjoyed this time with my family and friends, and I wasn't sure that I wanted to give it up for six months.

I distinctly recall lying in bed one Sunday morning, contemplating my core values. There I was—a holistic lifestyle coach that was actively coaching people on how to do a proper cleanse—yet I hadn't participated in one myself. I caught myself flirting with excuses and entertaining negative internal dialogues aimed at supporting my status quo. To say the least, I began to feel a bit hypocritical. That was the last straw. It was time to act.

I jumped out of bed and practically sprinted into the bathroom to find my wife getting ready for the day. In a state of utter certainty, I opened my mouth and proclaimed boldly, "I am *all in!*"

She gave me a puzzled look and said, "What are you talking about, crazy boy!"

I chose to remain silent with a grin on my face. She knew that I had been flirting with the idea of a cleanse for quite some time, and after a few more seconds of silence, she knew exactly what I was talking about.

Initially, she was a bit skeptical. One after another, she belted out probing questions, such as, "Do you know how expensive this will be?" "Are you going to have the time for food prep?" "What makes you think you can do this for a full six months?" In essence, she was bewildered by my all-or-nothing mentality. Clearly annoyed, she said, "So, just like that, huh? Six months of drastically altering your diet and energy levels, just like that?"

I knew that her questions and intentions were well intentioned, but I wanted to make a bold statement, so I snapped my fingers in a slightly flippant nature and stated, "Just like that." Being the great person that she is, she smiled, knowing that I wasn't going to be persuaded out of my determined state. She gave me a hug and supported me through the entire process.

My cleansing protocol went as planned, and as a bonus, it became one of the most empowering and rewarding experiences of my life. In fact, I have already resolved to make cleansing a regular part of my life. Looking back, I can clearly see the many important factors that helped me through that often-difficult experience. Chief among these factors was my undisputed power of focus. This single attribute has enhanced every area of my life and has allowed me to live the life of my choosing.

I now want to show you how to harness and organize this undeniable force into your own life, so that you can begin to more powerfully exorcise your excuses. By implementing the following steps, you'll undoubtedly reap the ever-powerful benefits of genuine focus.

Steps to Harnessing the Power of Focus

Step 1: Create a Crystal-Clear Vision (CCV)

Think of an area in which you feel successful. Don't be shy here! It could be anything from finances to your relationships to your career. My question to you is this: How did you get there, and what did it take to make that area of your life successful?

If you give yourself a moment to ponder these questions, I'm sure you'll come up with many good answers that are *crystal clear* to you. It's likely that your experience went a little something like this: You formulated a *vision* of what you wanted to achieve, and your vision was crystal clear. It wasn't nebulous or abstract. With your vision in mind, you mapped out a plan of attack so you could achieve your goals. You then acted on your plan by aggressively going after your goals with a focused intensity that nothing short of an act of God could deter you from.

Now let's slide to the opposite end of this mental spectrum. Look at an area of your life that you aren't so proud of. Don't be shy or prideful here, because we all have areas of weakness that need improvement. This might be an area of your life that you genuinely want to improve but have a hard time acting on. For example, let's say you keep telling yourself that you'd like to get into better shape and enhance your health.

> In the successful areas of your life, you possess a crystal-clear vision of what you want and why you want it. This is precisely why you excel at that area. This, my friend, is your golden key. Once you know what you want and why you want it, you can activate hidden forces within you. These innate forces compel you to action and drive you toward your vision.

At the surface, this may sound like a noble intention, and indeed it is. An unforeseen problem stems from the fact that your brain doesn't have a clue what "get in shape" or "get healthy" means. Sure, you may have a vague idea, and you may even take it a step further by imagining yourself as a skinnier version of you. But let's be real here. Do you even know what you're aiming for?

What does "get healthy" mean to you? Does it mean you become skinny or muscular, wear a certain jean size, or have washboard abs? Will you have constant energy? Will you have a lack of disease? What will your nutrition look like? Again, what exactly does health and fitness look like to you?

Okay, enough of the negative. Let's go back to the successful area of your life. It is here that you can answer these questions with clarity and certainty. The reason for this is very simple. In the successful area of your life, you possess a crystal-clear vision of what you want and why you want it. This is precisely why you excel at that area. This, my friend, is your golden key. Once you know what you want and why you want it, you can activate hidden forces within you. These innate forces compel you to action and drive you toward your vision.

To make sense of this, here are some steps that will help simplify the process:

A. Define and Clarify Your Core Values

Your core values are the values you cherish and hold dear to your heart despite challenging circumstances. Defining your core values is crucial in defining your purpose and identity. For example, most people have formed core values around education. As a society, one of our core value is that each person get an education despite any adversity. Think of it for a moment: do you want to spend thousands of dollars on tuition, be under stress for years, and attend classes that don't interest you?

We persist in our educational efforts despite the aforementioned adversities because we understand that the long-term benefits outlast the short-term discomfort. In like fashion, you must define your core values based on what I call your inner knowing.

For example, if one of your core values is to treat people as equals and with respect, your CCV should be written in alignment with this value. If you take a moment to listen to your soul, you might be amazed by what you learn. This is your inner knowing.

Keep in mind that you'll need to define your core values in many areas of your life. To point you in the right direction, consider the following areas:

- spiritual (your relationship to God or a higher power)
- mental/emotional
- educational
- financial
- health and fitness
- social
- self time (How much time do you need to be alone to ponder and process on a daily basis?)

- nutritional
- relationships and team building
- honesty/integrity
- career/work

These are just a few of the many areas of your life that need value clarification. It's impossible to advance toward your dreams and ambitions without clarifying your values because they act as your compass and your destination. Your core values serve as your bull's-eye. They enable you to focus because they provide you with something to focus on.

> It is impossible to advance toward your dreams and ambitions without clarifying your values because they act as your compass and your destination.

Here's an example. Part of my CCV reads, "I value whole organic foods in my diet. Therefore, I will not eat processed foods beyond one meal per week for my weekly cheat meal." I go on to clarify *why*: "I always treat my body with the utmost respect and care. It is deserving of the best that Mother Nature can offer—namely, whole organic foods and pure water." Here you can see that I have stated my core value and backed it up with a powerful *why*. (We will discuss the power of having a powerful and compelling *why* in the next chapter.)

B. State *Exactly* What You Want and Why You Want It

Are you ready for the fun part? Here you get to answer the question "What do you want?" Many of the people I've coached over the years have focused so much time on what they don't want that they've forgotten what they do want. To help jump-start your brain, imagine that you're eating at a high-end buffet with endless variety. *What* would you select for your meal, and *why* would you select it?

When you begin the process of defining and clarifying your core values, your heart will tell you what you desire. Keep in mind that I don't say this figuratively. The heart has the highest electromagnetic field of any part of your body. Your heart both senses and generates energy and thus is the organ that you can always turn to for guidance and help. Your heart and your brain together are the organs of intuition, so they should be used in defining and clarifying your core values.

This is why so many successful entrepreneurs and leaders attribute their success to "gut feeling." In truth, they're mistaking their gut for the electromagnetic yearnings and desires of their heart. Because the gut itself feels the energy emissions of the heart, it can easily be mistaken for your true compass.

When you're searching for what you want out of life, be sure that you not only think about what you want but also sense the ever-present desires of your heart. Jeff Olsen, one of my mentors and the author of *I Knew Their Hearts* has famously stated, "Energy never lies." Your heart emits your own emotional energy and keeps you in alignment with your inner truths. It should never be ignored, because it literally can't lie.

If you want to truly excel in any area of your life, honor your feelings and write them into your CCV. Remember you're standing at the buffet of life, and your responsibility is to select the best that life can possibly offer.

> Your heart and your brain together are the organs of intuition, so they should be used in defining and clarifying your core values.

Keep in mind that you never want to leave out your why. When you identify your why, it will stir your heart with passion and resonate with your mind. When defining your core values and stating what you want in life, ask yourself the golden question: Why? For example, why do you want to eat better? Why do you want a better job? Why do you want to stay physically fit? If the answer to any of these questions doesn't elicit a powerful emotional response within you, rest assured that you haven't yet found your true why.

Let's go back to my nutrition example. My core value was consuming organic whole foods in my diet. My why came as a direct result of my personal belief that my body is a temple that came from my Creator. Therefore, my why drives me to consume the cleanest food that Mother Nature offers. My why literally stirs my soul when I think about it, and it inspires me to daily action. I can assure you that your whys will create the same passion and inspiration in your heart.

> Your heart emits your own emotional energy and keeps you in alignment with your inner truths. As such, it should never be ignored, because it literally can't lie.

I must confess that I have a sweet tooth, and you can find me pounding some ice cream during my weekly cheat meal. Sometimes my sweet tooth tries to get the best of me on a day that doesn't include my cheat meal, and I'm tempted to turn my back on my nutritional core values. When this happens, I need only to think back to my why and experience the powerful emotions that it always brings. This not only puts an end to my temptation, it also reminds me that my why is of far greater value than the temporary pleasure of violating my core value.

The fact is that we human beings experience times of weakness. We commonly experience the temptation to live beneath our true potential or our Higher Self. In moments of stress and temptation, we can easily and conveniently forget our core values. During these moments, we must always recall our why. When we do, we place ourselves in an emotional and energetic state that's conducive to wise decision making.

C. State Your Intentions in the Present

When writing your CCV, phrase your desires in the present tense. Doing so has a profound effect on the reprogramming of your subconscious mind. It's vitally important to remember that your subconscious mind works only in the present—in the "now." It can't delineate the past or the future, as this is the function and duty of your conscious mind.

When crafting your CCV, never use phrases such as "I will be" or "When I," because your subconscious mind won't be able to manifest your intentions.

This is because you're *consciously* fixed on the future, an element that's foreign to your subconscious mind.

Here's an example of how *not* to write your CCV: "I will strive to be my ideal bodyweight of two hundred pounds. I will accomplish this in six months as I make better nutritional choices. I will eat healthier foods, and I will steer clear of junk food and soda pop." Please notice that this person was using all sorts of "I will" and "when I" statements, which are future oriented.

Here are those same intentions in the present tense: "I enjoy sitting at a healthy two hundred pounds. I feel confident and appreciative of the way that I look and feel. I enjoy eating healthy foods and limiting my processed food intake to no more than one small serving a day."

> When crafting your CCV never use phrases such as "I will be" or "When I," because your subconscious mind won't be able to manifest your intentions. This is because you're consciously fixed on the future, an element that is foreign to your subconscious mind.

In the latter example, the intentions were in the present tense though the writer's intentions were not yet a reality. By so doing, this person is actively reprogramming his subconscious mind to believe and act on what he's continually telling it. The dirty little secret is that your subconscious mind literally interprets your vividly imagined nowisms (yes, I made that word up) as your current reality. It begins to *believe* your programming because it's incapable of making value judgments based on truths or untruths. Once this happens, your actions will more naturally align with what you believe to be true. Remember—all action is belief oriented.

D. Add Passion, Inspiration, Enthusiasm, and Emotion

Did you know that the word *enthusiasm* comes from a phrase meaning "the God within"? In our Western culture, it's hard for us to grasp the essence of this statement because we've been conditioned to believe that we're subpar, dependent, and fully beholden to a higher power. While this may be true, we often fail to understand that we are part of this life-giving source. We possess the right and hold the responsibility to express this very sacred part of ourselves. When we do so, we create miracles within our own life. Alternatively, when we choose to ignore the divinity within us, we excuse away our inner greatness and squelch our ability to effect positive change.

This is your chance to enthusiastically express the God within you and thereby manifest your dreams and desires into your current reality. When you craft and read your CCV, be sure that you do so with passion and enthusiasm. When you do this, you'll automatically unleash emotion, or "energy-in-motion." When you live with enthusiasm, you unleash the God within and operate from your Higher Self.

As your subconscious mind mixes with energy-in-motion (emotion), it is profoundly and positively impacted. In this state of mind, your reprogramming efforts will be optimized and your behavior will follow suit.

Using this same principle, it's easy to see how people can become disenchanted, pessimistic, and cynical. Typically these people have invested so much negative energy in their subconscious mind that it has no other choice than to run a self-defeating, pessimistic program that sabotages them. They become the victim to their own negative programming. If you desire to exorcise your excuses, all self-defeating programs must be replaced before personal change can take place.

> We possess the right and hold the responsibility to express this very sacred part of ourselves. When we do so, we create miracles within our own life. Alternatively, when we choose to ignore the divinity within us, we excuse away our inner greatness and squelch our ability to effect positive change.

It's now time for you to awaken the God within you by writing a meaningful CCV. A great way to test the validity of your CCV is through the "goose bump test." This simply means your CCV is working to inspire you *if* you have goose bumps every time you read it. Goose bumps are a nervous system reaction often triggered by a high state of emotion. If you aren't getting goose bumps or feeling a high state of emotion while reading your CCV, you may need to infuse it with something that comes from your soul instead of your mind.

> When you live with enthusiasm, you're unleashing the
> God within and operating from your Higher Self.

E. Crystal Clear Means Crystal Clear

How many times have you been blessed with an inspiring idea, got excited about it, felt like you were going to act upon it, and then forgot about it? How does this happen? Where did the idea go? Are you just forgetful or lazy? The short answer is no.

Your brain craves what I call mental tangibility. It craves thoughts, ambitions, dreams, hopes, and desires that feel tangible to it. It does *not* like ambiguity, nebulousness, or gray areas as far as goal setting is concerned. The chance of forgetting such thoughts is extremely high because your brain can't latch onto them or can't identify with them, because they are nebulous and gray. When you give your brain tangible thoughts, forgetfulness is impossible, because these same thoughts now become part of *you*.

A key point to remember when crafting your CCV is that it should describe what you want your life to be like in actuality. Your CCV is the big-picture goal that you'll hereafter strive for. For this reason, it's paramount to give your brain the tangible "food" that it requires to take your dreams and turn them into reality. A few good questions to continually ask yourself are "Am I giving my brain clear instructions and corresponding pictures? Is my vision tangible? Can my brain latch onto the concepts and images that I am providing it with?"

As an example, consider this not-so-clear CCV snippet: "I am healthy and fit because I exercise regularly. I eat well and drink plenty of water. I like the way I feel, and I'm always striving to better myself. I enjoy my work, and my family life is satisfying and fulfilling."

Although this may sound good on the surface, it doesn't give the brain the tangible food it is so desperately desires. There's absolutely nothing here for your brain to latch onto, and as a consequence, your brain doesn't know *what* it's trying to achieve. So no action will be taken, because the statement is too ambiguous.

To make the statement more clear and tangible, the following questions need to be answered: What does health and fitness look like to you? What is plenty of water? How do you define regular exercise? What constitutes a satisfying and fulfilling family life? How do you feel? All these questions need to be answered with concrete details so that your brain has something to focus on. As Zig Ziglar famously stated, "If you aim at nothing, you will hit it every time."

Now let's contrast this with a snippet from a true CCV:

> I enjoy being healthy, fit, and physically attractive because of my exercise routine. I exercise six days a week and alternate my intensity based on how energetic I am feeling. I consume seventy ounces of fresh water each day, along with five servings of vegetables. Because of my habits, I feel good emotionally. I'm happy and cheerful and always choose to see the good in people. I enjoy my family life by spending quality time with them each and every day. I devote at least two hours to my family on weekdays and four hours on weekends.

Which one of these examples do you think your brain will latch onto? Which example provides the tangibility that's needed? The answer is obvious. When I present these contrasting examples to my students or clients, they often say something like, "Yeah, that all sounds good, but don't you think all those details are a little over the top?" I agree that it may sound like a lot of effort based on our socially contrived "I want it now" mentality, but I assure you that the latter example provides the crystal-clear detail that's absolutely necessary for personal change.

F. Keep It Real and Keep It *You*

When we get inspired and motivated, we naturally become driven to act on our goals. Hooray! This is a really good thing. The downside comes into focus when our excitement for change overtakes us. Our intentions can easily get hyper-inflated and flat-out unrealistic.

I have attended many personal development seminars over the years and have watched some of my peers bust out of the seminar with hyper-inflated goals that are obtuse, overstated, and worst of all, unattainable. They get pumped up, act on emotion, and throw their logic out the window. In so doing, they fail miserably and can't understand why.

As you can tell from reading this book, I'm all about reaching for the stars, but I'm also about being real with yourself. Remember you should be inspired, and you should stretch yourself—to a point. A good way to avoid this mess is to write down what you're truly *inspired* to write down. Inspiration comes from your heart and your right brain, which is your link to your Highest Self. You can access this wisdom in states of meditation, which I will cover in chapter 14.

If we aren't careful, our inspiration can be jaded or hijacked by our logical left brain. This problem can easily manifest in the pumped-up section of a seminar or motivational speaker. I'm all about these events and attend them myself, but if we aren't careful, our left brain can become overly logical and block out the messages that our Higher Self is trying to send through our right brain and through our heart.

Here's a good tip: After you write down your inspired intentions, give yourself a day to let your emotion simmer down. When this happens, it's time to apply a little logic to your vision.

For example, let's say you aren't musically gifted, and you choose to write that you are a concert pianist. This is a perfect example of allowing your ego to overtake your Higher Self. I understand that this may sound like an extreme example, but I can give you example after example of clients writing down financial, emotional, and other goals that are unrealistic for their current circumstances. Just remember this: if you're real with yourself, you'll find your sweet spot.

> Don't write your CCV to please your spouse, significant
> other, child, or anybody else. This does not make you selfish.
> In fact, it accomplishes quite the opposite by making you
> more mindful of your own needs. When you placate your
> own needs, you become empowered to serve others.

You must also keep in mind that your CCV is for *you* and nobody else. Don't write your CCV to please your spouse, significant other, child, or anybody else. This does not make you selfish. In fact, it accomplishes quite the opposite by making you more mindful of your own needs. When you placate your own needs, you become empowered to serve others.

This may sound contrary to our westernized values, but you must put yourself first so that you can therefore serve others. If you don't believe me, just look around at the millions of people in this country who give lopsidedly until there's nothing more to give. This often results in burnout and resentment toward those that are being served. It also results in a lack of mental, physical, emotional, spiritual, and social resources to accomplish the service that was originally intended.

I want to make one final point before we move on to the next chapter. When I say to keep your CCV *you*, I don't mean the you of the ego. Your ego has all sorts of labels that give you a false definition of who you are. Keep in mind that this isn't you're authentic self. The *you* that I speak of is your Higher Self, which knows what you need and will manifest it through your heart.

Well, my friend, we took an entire chapter to go over the first step of utilizing the enormous power of focus. According to personal development legend Napoleon Hill, only 2 percent of the population ever has. This puts you in exceptional company. In the next chapter, we'll learn how to transform your CCV into your reality.

CHAPTER 9

FROM CRYSTAL-CLEAR VISION TO CRYSTAL-CLEAR REALITY

Mixing Your Vision with Life-Changing Action

For as the body without the spirit is dead, so faith without works is dead also.
—James 2:26

When I was a young personal trainer and an aspiring entrepreneur, I was elated with the idea of corporate wellness. I wanted to help corporations cultivate healthy, fit, and vibrant employees who contributed to the well-being and bottom line of the company.

I remember going to bed at night, dreaming about the possibilities of working as a wellness coach for a large corporation. I wanted to make a name for myself and leave my footprint. My dreams slowly solidified into a vision as I continued to crystalize and refine my vision. I refined it to the point that I could nearly taste it. I had already taken the first step and made it real in my mind.

My problem wasn't with my CCV, because I had that nailed. It was with the next stage: action. I recall feeling like I'd done my part because I had met with a few businessmen who had been there and done that. I even met with a couple of companies to present my halfhearted plan. But I hadn't taken the time to make a well-thought-out business plan. My halfhearted effort forced the Life Teacher to intervene and teach me a very valuable lesson: a vision without a strategic plan is worthless and often painful.

My painful moments came while sitting in numerous HR offices being grilled by managers about my program. They wanted answers to questions that my program couldn't provide. I tried to regurgitate what my business buddies had told me, but the truth became painfully clear to me. I hadn't done my homework or taken the time to create a value-based wellness program that would fuel my dream of helping others. I vividly remember leaving those offices feeling stupid, embarrassed, and rejected.

> My halfhearted effort forced the Life Teacher to intervene
> and teach me a very valuable lesson: a vision without
> a strategic plan is worthless and often painful.

In this chapter, I want to accomplish two objectives: to show you what a quality crafted CCV looks like and to show you how to make effective SMART goals that will demand action from you.

Here is my disclaimer before we get started: This isn't meant for the faint of heart. If you tend to start a million personal development projects but fail to complete them, I invite you to change your paradigm and your resolve right now. What you're about to do will require disciplined thinking, creativity, and most importantly *action*.

Remember you're reading a book that gives you a step-by-step plan for exorcising your excuses. This is one of the most important and fundamental steps that you'll ever take, so if you're ready to roll, let's get started.

Imagine you're a gold miner of the forty-niners era. You have traveled far and packed your brain with images of gold that will make you wealthy beyond belief. This story can be likened to your CCV. It contains the details of *what* you'll receive when you claim your prize. In your case, your CCV gives you a clear picture of what your life will look like.

Your CCV doesn't elaborate on *how* you're going to get to the gold. It doesn't give you a strategy or the tools you'll use to mine the gold, what trails to take, and what equipment will be necessary to achieve your vision. This is the role of goals.

Below is the difference between the role of a CCV and the role of a goal:

> ➤ Crystal-Clear Vision (CCV) is the end result of what you envision and dream of. This is your *what*.
> ➤ Goals are your *how*. They include strategies and tactics that you'll use to obtain your CCV. Goals also clarify the resources needed to accomplish your goal.

Before we get to the how of goal setting, I want to give you an example of what a quality CCV looks like. Keep in mind that a CCV can be short, long, or anything in between. Just be sure to follow the guidelines I presented to you in the previous chapter.

I've chosen to share my own CCV with you. I admit that I've hesitated to do this because it discloses some of my deepest desires and passions. But I have nothing to hide. Please know that this is only an example, so don't get offended by desires. It's your desires that matter, and they're waiting to be discovered.

My Crystal-Clear Vision
Spiritual

I wake up every day feeling grateful for the wonderful life that I have been richly blessed with. I commune with my Higher Self every morning, and I seek to express the divine within me on a moment-to-moment basis. I am spiritually fulfilled, and I live presently. I remember the divine being that I truly am, and I help others understand and see that same gift. This is one of my greatest callings in this life, and I am passionate about it. I cherish the opportunity to better myself each and every day by applying the things that I have been blessed to learn.

I take time for myself through meditation, prayer, introspection, and adequate rest. This allows me to remain present and "in-spirit" so that I can powerfully influence and help others. I am a divine instrument, and I seek to help others in any way that I can without judgment or resentment. By living presently, I live an inspired life, and I maintain an intimate relationship with my creator and become unified with this power. I operate from my Highest Self and recognize the simple beauty that life truly is. Because of my intimate relationship with my divine Source, I am blessed to influence the lives of others in a profound way.

I live a life of humble gratitude, and I am quick to reclaim my Highest Self when my ego takes over and tries to dictate who I am. I sense, I feel, and I trust my Highest Self into the paths that God has intended me to walk. I never follow the crowd, and I challenge norms that are inherently contrary to the inner whisperings of my soul.

Business

Lifelong Fitness Inc. is constantly evolving into a premier and sought-after Holistic Lifestyle Coaching and Fitness Center. The services provided are truly inspiring, life changing, and revolutionary. We are bold in our approach but always loving and respectful of our clients. We provide a culture of nonjudgment, empathy, unconditional love, and caring. Lifelong Fitness is growing and expanding exponentially on an annual basis.

Sugar Freedom Revolution is taking the online world by storm. I am an in-demand public speaker for many companies and hold privately held events on the side. Nothing in this world thrills me more than being able to use the bully pulpit to spread the message of mental and physical health. I feel exhilarated and passionate as I present my masterpiece seminars multiple times per week.

I am an engaging and sought-after online businessman. SFR is growing exponentially and providing me with a platform to live out my true calling in life. I network daily with online business owners and my presence as a thought leader is growing daily. I enjoy the professional relationships that I am privileged to have with my business partners. I thrive on the synergy that we create together.

I am continually creating new classes, providing new services, and writing new books. I work with experienced mentors to help me along the way. I express my creative genius through this medium and fulfill the archetype of author, speaker, caretaker, and business owner.

Finances

I am blessed to be financially secure and independently wealthy. I have complete freedom over my time. Words cannot express how grateful I am for money that I have earned. My money allows me to spend time with my family and spend at least twenty hours with my kids on a daily basis. I work hard when I want to, and I love it. Conversely, I play hard when I want to, and I enjoy every minute of it because my business is a self-sustaining moneymaking machine that grows stronger and wealthier each and every day.

I am rich, and I love it. I am compassionate and giving to all those who are deserving of my help. I feel blessed that I am able mentor those who are as ambitious and hungry as I am. I love the feeling of money pouring into my bank account. It almost feels like a dream, but it is my reality, and I have earned it in every conceivable way. I am grateful that my hard work and persistence has paid off and yielded me a life of financial independence and freedom to enjoy the things I care most about.

I feel blessed to know that I have provided my family a life of financial independence. Because of this, I am able to focus on the most important things, such as spiritual, emotional, and social development with my kids. Taryn and I could not be happier. We enjoy our lifestyle of privilege, and we count our blessings on a daily basis. We are growing closer together as a family by spending time together each and every day. My family is my main priority and everything is secondary to them. My life truly is blessed, and I am grateful to the opportunity to live it to its potential. Life truly is good!

Please note that my CCV includes different areas of my life, such as spiritual and financial. For the record, I chose not to include some because of length. Notice that my CCV followed all the guidelines in the previous chapter. I can honestly say that I still get chills when I read it.

As I pasted my CCV into this book, I realized it's time for an update. I wrote this version about two years back, and I have fulfilled many of the areas that I wrote about. It's wise to view your CCV as a breathing and living document that will change as your vision becomes your reality.

In addition, your CCV may need to change when you experience what I call a CCV heart transplant. This happens when your heart begins to lead you in a different direction than what is currently stated in your CCV. You may experience confusion when this happens and ask yourself, *Am I not being true to my CCV?* In reality, your desires can and should change as you advance through your life.

You may have noticed that in the financial subheading of my CCV, I was very bold in my desire to make a lot of money. Many would perceive this as pretentious, arrogant, or even worldly, but keep in mind that one of the steps in the last chapters advises you to "keep it real and keep it you."

I was raised in a financially conservative household where money was viewed and used from a mentality of scarcity. Through my reprogramming efforts, I've been able to undo a lot of programming that isn't conducive to making a good living. You may find areas in your CCV that make other people uncomfortable if they read it, but keep in mind that it's not about them; it's about you. If you're a private person, rest assured that you need not share your CCV with anybody.

Some elements of your CCV won't change. Examples include character issues, spiritual issues, and other constants that require a process rather than a destination. Updating your CCV is typically reserved for goals that have finish lines attached to them. For example, if you have a financial vision of making a certain salary and you achieve it, it may be appropriate to update it when you surpass your goal.

My CCV is fairly long and comprehensive because I want to become very clear on all areas of my life. Don't feel obligated to make yours long, elaborate, or fancy. Simply get something on paper and then revise it later. Remember it's a process that will evolve over time.

Below is a CCV of one of my former clients. It's shorter and much more to the point than mine, but it still embodies the elements of a great CCV. I've opted to print this CCV verbatim.

> I am so happy and grateful I've successfully applied the model of sustainability to all aspects of my physical (fitness), mental, and spiritual health and life. Today I'm better than I was one year ago. I live confidently in the present, look good in thirty-six-inch-waist pants, turn my wife on, feel free to express myself, can play sports with my kids, choose to eat healthily, regularly work out, see all things positively, empower and support my family in a way I never dreamed of before, and explore my deepest potential. I believe in what I'm doing and integrate my sense of purpose into who I am.

> I have a strategy for personal fitness that is about my long-term health and growth. I now arise at six thirty each morning and start my physical and mental day right. I exercise six times each week for thirty to forty-five minutes each day, starting at a quarter to seven. I maintain balance by alternating my workouts. I do resistance (weights) training three times each week and cardio training the other three days of the week. I track my food and am accountable for what I eat. I feel more energy and zest for life than I ever have before.

I live life with great passion and great love interlaced with fun and humor. Everyone who comes in contact with me leaves with the perception that I put the FU in fun and genuinely care. I listen more than I talk. I deeply love my family and strive to empower and support them. I lead by example. I have pride in myself both physically and in what I do for a living. I take care of my body by eating healthily, drinking water, sleeping, praying, walking, running, swimming, weight training, biking, and playing sports.

With these examples in mind, it's time for you to craft your own CCV. Start to collect your thoughts over the next few days, putting them down on paper. Then begin to organize them into an intelligently crafted CCV using the guidelines in the previous chapter.

It's now time to turn your *how* into your reality through the art and practice of goal setting. Your CCV, important as it is, serves only as the *what*. It's vitally important that you first craft your CCV and then follow it with intelligent goal setting. This follows a logical and linear sequence because your *what* should always precede your *how*, providing a clear target of what you're aiming for. It also serves as the launchpad for all your goal-oriented ideas.

You have likely tried goal setting before with mixed results. If you've tried and failed with goal setting or flat-out don't believe in goal setting, I can assure you that the steps I'm about to share will ensure a better experience for you if you're willing exorcise your excuses by taking action on them.

> Your CCV, important as it is, serves only as the what. It's vitally important that you first craft your CCV and then follow it with intelligent goal setting. This follows a logical and linear sequence because your *what* should always precede your *how*, providing a clear target of what you're aiming for.

At this point, you should at least have a rough draft of your Crystal-Clear Vision. With your CCV in mind, I'm now going to share with you the SMART goal-setting model that has been widely popularized in the last thirty years. SMART simply stands for the following:

specific

measurable

action oriented and accountability

realistic

time sensitive

Often people think that they're setting SMART goals, but one or more pieces are missing or misunderstood. This often creates confusion and frustration, so to prevent this, I want to take you through this process step by step, using a nutrition-related example.

Let's pretend that you want to decrease your sugar intake because your CCV has stated that you consume only one treat per day. Let's also assume that you're consuming anywhere from four to five treats per day. With this in mind, let's run this example through the SMART model and see what we come up with.

Step 1: Be Specific—*Very* Specific

Using our sugar goal, we could be specific by using this plan of attack:

> I will progressively cut down my sugar intake within six weeks. I am currently eating five treats per day, and I intend to consume no more than one by the end of six weeks. I will follow the schedule detailed below:

Week 1: Five treats per day, but I'll track my treats so I can elevate my awareness of my bad habit.

Week 2: Four treats per day.

Week 3: Three treats per day, and I won't have a treat after six in the evening. I also will eat less if I don't have the desire.

Week 4: Two treats per day.

Week 5: Two treats per day while aiming for one. If I don't feel the desire for treats, I will not partake out of habit.

Week 6: One treat per day if needed—and not to be consumed after six.

Definition of treat: No more than 150 calories of a processed or sugary food that is detrimental to my health. Anything man-made and nonnatural.

Tools and procedures needed: I'm going to use myfitnesspal. com to track my food on a daily basis.

Notice how detailed and specific this plan is. It's rock-star status! Here we've identified how many calories a treat constitutes, what time of day it's appropriate to eat the treat, and a no-nonsense weaning schedule that's very simple to understand. Furthermore, there's a stated time frame of six weeks to realize the goal.

It's important to remember that you don't have to make your goals complicated. The example above gives the brain just enough tangibility to know exactly what the target is and how to get there. The *S* of SMART goals is without question the most important part of the goal-setting process because it makes the rest of the process seamless.

Step 2: Be Able to Measure Your Goal

If you were specific in step 1, this next step will be easy for you. In the first step, I laid out a treat cessation schedule that clearly spelled out how many treats would be permissible during weeks 1 through 6. With this level of specificity, I'm now able to *measure* my progress on a daily and weekly basis.

> Regardless of the nature of your goal, you should have something to track your progress, so that you can measure it.

I recommend that you measure your goal at the same time at the conclusion of every day. A good time to do so is around nine at night, when you're winding down for the day. Sit down and look over your performance. As stated in step 1, you can use www.myfitnesspal.com or a similar tracking service to track your nutrition so you can indeed measure your goal accurately and effectively.

Regardless of the nature of your goal, have something to track your progress so you can measure it. How else are you going to know how you're doing? If you aren't a technically savvy person, manually track your nutrition or other goal so that you can accomplish this step of the SMART goal model.

Step 3: Three Very Important People to Be Accountable To

With nearly two decades of experience in the personal training and personal coaching industry, I can tell you without hesitation that accountability is one of the most overlooked elements of goal setting. Without accountability, your goals are nothing more than halfhearted wishes.

Most people believe that accountability means being accountable to somebody else. But this accounts for only one third of true accountability. Listed below are the three most important people that you must be accountable to:

A. Yourself

There's an old saying that states, "You can bullshit the fans, but you can never bullshit the players." You, my friend, are the player. You're playing the game of life, and within this game, you must honor an undeniable truth: You are the only person on this earth that can hold you accountable and enact change in your life. Nobody else can do it for you.

At this point, avoid slipping back into patterns of self-denial or delusion that are associated with conditioned beliefs. When it's time to sit down with yourself and account for your actions, you must be 100 percent honest with yourself. Imagine for a moment looking at your food tracking app and realizing that you have fallen short of your goal five out of the seven days of the week.

At this point, it's easy to go into a state of denial and start making excuses. You may find yourself using internal dialogues similar to the following: "Well, I was really busy, and life threw me so many curve balls that I will just have to start again next week." No, no, no! This excuse-laden mind-set plunges you straight into a state of delusion. You are, in essence, denying that you missed your goal (though you did) and deluding yourself that you had no control over it. It may be hard for you to hear these brutal facts, but rest assured that these forms of internal dialogues are excuse making at its finest because they give you a false sense of justification.

This is not to say that you should beat yourself up or be hard on yourself. It's actually time for the exact opposite. *This is a time to look at the situation for what it is, learn from it, and then move forward.* Effective questions to ask might be "What caused me to fall short of my goal, and what can I do about it in the future?" or "How can I prepare more effectively this week so that I don't fall short next week?" These and similar questions will help you understand what's necessary in the future to ensure success.

B. A Lovingly Honest Loved One

A lovingly honest loved one will shoot straight with you and tell you the way it is. He or she will voice it in a manner that preserves your dignity and feelings. This is the person that won't let you off the hook by using apologetic statements such as, "Yeah, I know it's tough, and I don't blame you for having more cookies. I would, too, if I had that much going on in my life." People who make excuses for us do nothing to empower us; rather, they do a lot to enable us. In the end, we feel a false sense of justification because "somebody cares." Reality then sets in as we realize we haven't moved an inch toward our goal.

Find somebody who would say this: "I love you too much to allow you to make excuses for yourself." Meet with this person daily, if possible—or weekly as a minimum. Be sure that her or she is 100 percent clear on your goals, intentions, and strategies so that he or she can ask the right questions and keep you in check when you're tempted to make excuses.

Finally, select somebody that operates on the same spiritual plane as you. Your beliefs should be similarly aligned so that you can communicate in a language that will be mutually understood. Be sure that you naturally resonate with this person and feel comfortable sharing personal information with him or her.

C. A Coach or Expert

This element of accountability is often ignored. If you are to rid yourself of excuse making and hasten lasting change, it's absolutely necessary to be accountable to an expert in the field of your desired change. For example, if you're focusing on what you eat, it would be wise to meet with a nutritionist that could not only hold you accountable but also help you understand what to be accountable for.

Regardless of the area of your life that you desire to change, there's always a well-qualified coach who can help you know what to shoot for and how to accomplish it. By so doing, you'll minimize your risk of wasting time and striving for unrealistic or unobtainable goals.

Be sure to select a coach or expert that will hold your feet to the flames and make sure you're progressing toward your goal. Ideally, select somebody who has a good working balance of compassion and boldness. This balance is important so that he or she can shoot it to you straight and see through your excuses or delusions. Don't worry! We all have them, and that's why a coach is so valuable.

> If you are to rid yourself of excuse making and hasten lasting change in your life, it's absolutely necessary to be accountable to an expert in the field of your desired change.

Be sure to report to your three very important people regularly. I've found that the following reporting schedule works best for most people:

> *Personal accountability* (you): Report to yourself daily. Evening is best because your daily responsibilities have come to an end, and you have some free time to think and reflect without distraction.

> *Accountability to a loved one*: Make this daily, if possible. If you don't have the luxury of checking in daily, try for at least one or two times per week. Be sensitive to their time and schedule, but know that they will likely be willing to check in with you daily if their schedule permits. To be respectful of their times, try to keep your accountability sessions to fifteen minutes.

Step4: Keep Your Goals Real—Very Real!

When I help clients set goals, I often notice that they're excited to change their lives in the moment and therefore write over-the-top goals. I spoke of a few parallel points concerning your CCV in chapter 8 under the subhead "Keep It Real and Keep It You," so please review if necessary.

As a caring coach, I often advise clients to reconsider their goals. However, in their excitement they don't shoot for the stars, they shoot beyond them. In the moment, this always feels very good to them because they're sure they can accomplish their lofty goals. Unfortunately, these same people end up realizing that reality doesn't line up with their cosmic goals.

Allow me to share a few guidelines that will help you set realistic goals.

First, select a goal that will stretch you. When you act on a goal that stretches you beyond your normal comfort level, your conscious mind is forced into a state of awareness. This is a prerequisite for subconscious reprogramming for one very simple reason: you can't override a subconscious program that you're unaware of.

When you stretch yourself beyond your normal limits by acting on your goals, your subconscious mind takes note of your newfound behavior and essentially asks you, "Is this your new normal? Shall I write a new program and replace your old program?"

It's often forgotten that the conscious mind is responsible for reprogramming the subconscious mind. When you consciously introduce a new action into your life and repeat it over a length of time, your subconscious mind finally yields to the commands of the conscious mind and says, "It looks like my master has made it clear that a new program needs to be installed. So be it!"

Your conscious mind is analogous to a general directing a large army. His army is large and powerful, but a single person is ultimately commanding it. In your case, your small conscious mind is the general that's directing the programming of your enormously powerful subconscious mind.

Recall a time that you saw this play out in your own life, a time that you changed a lifestyle trait for the better. Initially you likely had an internal dialogue that sounded similar to the following: "I really like the concept of changing my eating habits, but I never thought in a million years that it would be this hard. I don't know how much longer I can take this." After making healthy food choices over and over, you likely found yourself saying the opposite: "Well, this is not so bad after all. I feel better, and I actually like healthy food much better than the junk I was eating."

This same pattern will play out when you select a goal that stretches you. You'll likely feel uncomfortable for a short period, but, given enough repetition, your newfound habit will become second nature to you.

Second, you must not overstretch yourself. This may seem contradictory to my first guideline of stretching yourself, so please allow me to explain. When you stretch yourself, you induce a certain state of positive stress, but too much of a good thing can quickly turn disastrous. There is an art form that takes time to master. You must know how much to stretch yourself without crossing the line. Getting closer to the line incurs a positive form of stress. When you cross the line, you incur excessive or negative stress.

The art of this technique is to get close to the line but never cross it. Let common sense be your guide. Don't let your emotions dictate a goal that's unrealistic. Use your left brain to reason it out and your right brain to sense it. You'll know that you've struck gold when you get to the end of your day and feel worked and stretched, but not worn out and defeated.

When you stretch yourself, you'll likely find yourself hosting an internal dialogue that says, "Today was hard, but I'm sure glad I held strong. I feel good about myself, and my self-confidence is growing."

> Don't let your emotions dictate a goal that's unrealistic. Use your left brain to reason it out and your right brain to sense it. You'll know that you've struck gold when you get to the end of your day and feel worked and stretched, but not worn out and defeated.

When you cross the line, you'll host an internal dialogue like this: "I'm so glad the day is over. I'm stressed out, and I can only hope I can maintain this intensity level tomorrow, but I seriously doubt it." When you cross the line, you'll likely fail at your goals, further depressing your efforts. This is why it's crucial to learn the art of "stretching but not stressing."

Step 5: Put a Fuse on Your Goals

If I were your college professor, and I gave you a ten-thousand-word report due at the end of the semester, when would you complete your report? Statistically, it's almost guaranteed that you would complete it very close to the deadline. In contrast, what if I told you that the paper was due in three weeks and that it was worth 25 percent of your grade? Do you think you would get the paper done a little faster?

This, my friend, is known as Parkinson's law, and it can have a profound impact on your ability to follow through on your goals. Parkinson's law states, "Work expands to fill the time available for its completion." Knowing the innate wisdom of this timeless principle, it's important to set appropriate deadlines for your goals. Depending on the nature of your goal, you may need to set multiple deadlines to accommodate long-term, midrange, and short-term goals.

A simple example of this can be seen in step 1, where I illustrated a treat-cessation plan. When setting a simple goal like this, there's no reason to set long, medium, or short-term goals. With more complex goals, such as starting a business, you would want to spell out goal deadlines clearly. A simple example may look like the following:

Long-Term Goal

open organic restaurant called Griff's Grub by _____ (fill in realistic date)

Intermediate Goals

- business plan completed by _____
- business/investment partners finalized and legalized by _____
- funding completed by _____
- equipment purchased by _____
- location secured and leased by _____

Short-Term Goals

- inquire about Small Business Administration loan by _____
- start on business plan on _____
- begin market research and have it completed by _____

The style and fashion of your deadlines will vary depending on the nature and length of your goal, but be sure to have this crucial detail in your plan of attack. This will require more work, but it will draw that proverbial line in the sand and enact the awesome power of Parkinson's law.

Standards versus Goals: Now or Later?

It's time for me to backtrack just a little, but don't worry—because it's a strategic and timely backtrack.

As I've mentioned numerous times, the subconscious mind works only in the here and now. It's concerned with what we're experiencing right here and right now, and it doesn't have the ability to dig into our past. That's the responsibility of your conscious mind. When I say the word *goal*, where does your mind go? Does it go to the future, or does it work in the now?

The answer is obvious. When most of us hear the word *goal*, we think of something future oriented. A goal is something we desire but are not yet living. This can present a problem for our subconscious mind because it works only in the now. With this in mind, the very word *goal* can be problematic for the subconscious mind because it casts your desired behavior into the future. Your subconscious can't run a future-oriented program. To avoid a subconscious snafu, get your goals into the present.

The solution to this perceived conundrum is to set standards rather than goals. Why? Because standards denote who you are right now—not in the future. So when setting your goals, I invite you to view them through a slightly different lens. Don't set goals; set *standards*.

Using our previous SMART example of limiting the intake of treats, you would identify each weekly goal as a standard rather than as a goal. For example, you would write the following standard: "This week, I'm consuming only two treats per day." This is your standard, and it is not to be broken. If it's merely a goal, it's future oriented and can't be used to reprogram your now-oriented subconscious mind. Furthermore, when you set a standard for yourself, you also set a corresponding expectation for yourself.

Don't set goals; set standards.

If it's merely a goal, it's future oriented and can't be used to reprogram your now-oriented subconscious mind.

In the next chapter, we'll learn about time-tested techniques for exorcising your excuses. We're going to dig deep into your mind and your soul so that you can start manifesting the life that you were meant to live.

CHAPTER 10

EXCUSE EXORCISM 1

Unlocking Your Inner Greatness through
Physical Awareness and Expression

Let us not look back in anger, nor forward in fear, but around in awareness.
—James Thurber

Have you ever felt somebody? Before your mind goes to the gutter, know that I'm not talking about physically feeling somebody. I'm talking about that person in your life who exudes a positive energy that you can literally feel. Maybe you've walking into a room and immediately felt one of these people. They're the ones who are typically upbeat and focus on the positive things in life. They have bad days and get into bad moods, as we all do, but they enjoy life, smile a lot, and are tremendously productive with their time, resources, and relationships.

While teaching one of my first seminars years ago to a local crowd, in walked a stranger named Mike, whom my sister had referred. She jokingly told Mike, "You need to meet my little brother, Griff, because he is just as weird and as upbeat as you are." As Mike walked in the door, he had a big grin on his face, as though he had known me for years; in fact, we had never met. He gave me a big hug as his formal introduction. I remember feeling the energy in the room distinctively shift as he walked in. It was as if somebody had grabbed the energy dial in the room and cranked it up a notch or two.

I later partnered with Mike for a time to present our seminars to various local companies. To this day, I'm intrigued by his insatiable desire to see the good in people and to live in a passionate and caring way. He takes pleasure in the simple things of life and is a devoted student of personal development. He is cheerful, nonjudgmental, and innately connected to his spiritual self.

In stark contrast, we all know "that person" that seems to suck the very life out of us when we're forced to interact with him or her. As I mentioned in chapter 2, Linda was this person for me. Every time I met with her, I felt forced to perform mental gymnastics just to stay positive. Linda had an excuse for everything and chose to see the world as a dire place, filled with misery, failure, and disappointment. She lived a life of constant pessimism and defaulted to the lowest and most common mentality, which states, "It's just the way life is."

To this day, Linda and Mike are running programs in their subconscious minds that have determined their current reality. Here's a question I'd like you to ponder: How can two people be so different? On the surface, one would guess they come from two very different worlds. Are they different because of happenstance? Do they have different fates? Is their upbringing dictating their current reality? As I have clearly taught with the Perception Reality Model, these factors do play a role, but they don't have the power to control destiny.

It might interest you to know that Mike was raised in what many people would consider a harsh environment. After his parents divorced while he was young, he started smoking, among other things. He also became a rabble-rouser and a troublemaker. His parents didn't love or nurture him, as parents should. Specifically, he wasn't nourished with spiritual or religious teachings, and he enjoyed little to no structure. Mike was forced to fend for himself from an early age, which was the genesis of his entrepreneurial nature.

It may further interest you to know that Linda was raised in conditions that were the antithesis of Mike's. Her family was well off financially. She received religious and spiritual training and was well loved by her parents and siblings. She received a good education, earning her master's degree in marketing, and was gainfully employed at the time of our coaching.

So I ask you the same question: how can these two people be so different? In this very important chapter, I'll explain how we create our own inner universe and will illuminate how that universe creates and influences our psychology and our physiology. My intention is to teach you how to operate from your Higher Self so you can leave the other part of you—the doubting, pessimistic, excuse-making part of you—in the past where it belongs.

Abiding by the Laws of Energy

Consider this mind-bender: we are nothing more than big bundles of intelligently organized energy. This is scientifically verified down to the atomic and subatomic level. Everything in this world is energy. With this in mind, it's important to know that everything has a vibration because it is all energy. This is always true, regardless of whether we're talking about a metal baseball bat or a silky feather.

It's vitally important to realize that each and every one of our thoughts, words, emotions, and deeds carries with it a specific energy pattern and vibratory rate. Our job as human beings is to harness and direct positive energy for our good and for the good of humanity.

> We are nothing more than big bundles of intelligently organized energy.

> Our job as human beings is to harness and direct positive energy for our good and for the good of humanity.

Mike did a much better job than Linda at harnessing and directing positive energy into his being. Because of his *mental and physical lifestyle habits*, he was able to harness high vibrating or positive energy that was beneficial to him. In contrast, Linda also harnessed energy, but it came from a much lower vibrational source. We typically call this type of energy "negative," because it has the ability to impact life negatively.

William Ernest Henley, in his famous poem "Invictus," wrote, "I am the master of my fate, / I am the captain of my soul." Little did he know that he was correct in a literal sense. Little did he know that his spoken truth had everything to do with the proper channeling of positive energy.

Let's make this very simple to understand. If you allow and appropriately channel positive energy into your life, you will build the life that your Source (or God) intended you to live. If you allow and channel negative energy into your life, you will build an average or mediocre life that falls short of your divine potential.

> It's vitally important to realize that each and every one
> of our thoughts, words, emotions, and deeds carries
> with it a specific energy pattern and vibratory rate.

You are the magician of your own life, a magician who has nearly unlimited power. This power can be used to channel energy for your dream life or for a life of mediocrity. The choice is yours, and it *is* that simple. By simple, I don't mean easy, because life always sends learning opportunities that may seem difficult and undesirable at the moment, but with the proper channeling of energy, you will *always* emerge as the victor and gain wisdom in the meantime.

> If you allow and appropriately channel positive energy
> into your life, you will build the life that your Source
> (or God) intended you to live. If you allow and channel
> negative energy into your life, you will build an average or
> mediocre life that falls short of your divine potential.

All the methodologies and principles I teach are rooted in the self's energy management, or the flow of positive or negative energy in your own life.

You become the magician and the master of your fate. This is where you begin to exorcise your excuses through harnessing positive energy that allows you to live as your Highest Self.

You and you alone create resistance to your inner greatness by swimming in undesirable energy patterns. These patterns can be physical, mental, nutritional, or verbal in nature. They compromise your inner greatness by creating the illusion that mediocrity is normal and acceptable.

We often validate these feelings by looking around us and comparing ourselves to people who aren't aware of their Highest Self. I am in no way suggesting that they are bad or weak people; they are just ignorant of what they are truly capable of. Any time we aren't living from our Highest Self, we're living in a state of mediocrity. In this state, we excuse away our inner greatness, which manifests through our Highest Self. Seen from this perspective, is it any wonder so many of us become experts at excuse making?

> Any time we aren't living from our Highest Self, we're living in a state of mediocrity. In this state, we excuse away our inner greatness, which manifests through our Highest Self.

The following excuse exorcisms need to be performed in their entirety if the Highest Self is to reign supreme.

Excuse Exorcism 1: Getting E-*motion*-al

Now that we know we're nothing more than big walking bundles of intelligently organized energy, it behooves us to direct it intelligently. Jeff Olsen, author of *I Knew Their Hearts* and a personal mentor of mine once told me that emotion is energy in motion. Wow! This was so profound for me, yet so loaded with common sense.

If emotion is energy in motion, and positive energy has a high vibration, it stands to reason that we need to direct our emotions through getting in motion. This is done by attending to the following:

-   the way you walk (pace, tempo, intensity)
-   the way you breathe
-   the way you exercise your body
-   your posture (guarded or upright)
-   your tone of voice

If you're scratching your head right now, wondering how these attributes will help you exorcise your excuses, please allow me to explain. When you move your body, you begin to move chemicals and hormones in your body that are partially responsible for your physical and mental well-being.

Science has shown us that when we exercise, we balance mood-regulating neurotransmitters in our brain. In general, these neurotransmitters are norepinephrine, dopamine, and serotonin, which play a huge role in how we feel physically, mentally, spiritually, and emotionally.

> If emotion is energy in motion, and positive energy has
> a high vibration, it stands to reason that we need to
> direct our emotions through getting in motion.

With this in mind, answer a very simple question: Are you going to feel motivated or inspired to improve your life if you're feeling physically and mentally drained, moody, and irritable? The irrefutable truth that we must accept is that our bodies are hardwired to exercise and to move. Through movement and exercise, we bring ourselves into a positive state of e-*motion*.

In this state, we become physiologically and psychologically amenable to change. We actually *want* to change. Surely at times you've sought change, but then found yourself wandering around the house with poor posture, not exercising, breathing shallowly, and feeling sorry for yourself. Is it any wonder you failed in your efforts? Is it possible that you were operating from your Highest Self in this state of mind? Of course not! You were reveling in a low-energy frequency that didn't have the power to inspire or enact change.

In his fascinating book *Spark: The Revolutionary New Science of Exercise and the Brain,* John J. Ratey, MD, describes in detail how exercise positively affects levels of depression, anxiety, and stress. Regarding exercise, he states,

> In addition to feeling good when you exercise, you feel good about yourself, and that has a positive effect that can't be traced to a particular chemical or area in the brain. If you've been feeling down and you start to exercise and feel better, the sense that you're going to be OK and that you can count on yourself shifts your entire attitude. The stability of the routine alone can dramatically improve your mood. Clearly, there's something going on.[4]

> Exercising your body helps regulate ADD, ADHD, addictions, and other physiological issues that might be barriers to your personal development.

He further illustrates how exercise mitigates and regulates ADD, ADHD, addiction, and hormonal balance in men and particularly women. So if you find yourself saying: "Well every time I try to make a change in my life, I run into _____ (fill in any of the above mentioned conditions), and it sabotages my efforts," just know that you can instantly employ the weapon of e-motion, which will help you overcome the influences of the aforementioned road blocks. Yes! I'm telling you that exercising your body helps regulate ADD, ADHD, addictions, and other physiological issues that might be barriers to your personal development.

Walking

Let's touch briefly on your gait pattern, or the way you walk. Think of a time in your life when things were smooth sailing and free flowing. How did you walk? Did you have an upright posture and a solid stride that showed confidence? I'm sure you did.

---

[4] John J. Ratey, MD, *Spark: The Revolutionary New Science of Exercise and the Brain* (New York: Little, Brown and Company, 2008).

Now contrast that with a time when you felt depressed or filled with anxiety. Chances are good that your shoulders slumped and your pace slowed to that of a snail. These two very different modes of walking perpetuate the very behavior that they personify. In other words, when you walk depressed, you feel depressed. Conversely, when you walk confidently, you feel confident.

> The act of walking briskly with an upright posture sends an undeniable message to both your conscious and subconscious mind that you are alive, confident, and capable of crafting your own life scenario despite your current circumstances.

Here is the take-home: When you don't feel like walking with confidence or with swagger, this is when you need it the most. The act of walking briskly with an upright posture sends an undeniable message to both your conscious and your subconscious mind that you are alive, confident, and capable of crafting your own life scenario despite your current circumstances. It literally changes your physiological state by elevating your energy to a higher level of vibration. In this positive state of energy, you can fend off excuse making and invite change.

Breathing

Paul Chek, founder of the prestigious CHEK Institute in San Diego, crafted a totem pole that illustrates the needs of our physical and spiritual being. This totem pole is ordered in a hierarchical level of importance, and sitting near the top is the function of breathing. Why is breathing so high on his physical and spiritual totem pole? As we all know, if we don't breathe, we die. We therefore can conclude that to breathe is to live, and to breathe correctly is to live optimally.

Dozens of practices and disciplines teach correct breathing patterns, and I highly recommend that you find a methodology that resonates with you. To keep things simple, just know that you need to breathe correctly to prevent undue stress in your body. Improper breathing patterns create elevated stress hormones, which activate your sympathetic nervous system—the part of your nervous system that tells you to go, go, go.

To breathe is to live, and to breathe correctly is to live optimally.

If you aren't breathing properly, you're setting yourself up for undue physiological stress. This typically comes with chest breathing. Proper breathing occurs when you breathe in through your nose and allow the air to fill your belly naturally first and your chest cavity second. In this sequence of breathing, you're using your diaphragm in a ratio of 75 percent belly breathing to 25 percent chest breathing. In other words, your chest should rise only during the last 25 percent of your inhalation.

Let's see how this plays out in real-life situations. When you become stressed, do you take deep diaphragmatic breaths through your nose that naturally fill your belly first and your chest last? Or do you take shallow and nervous chest breaths through your mouth? The former pattern of breathing eases stress, while the latter creates it.

If you wish to correct your breathing pattern, you must first become aware that your breathing has gone awry. A method I teach my clients is to wear a wristband or a bracelet that reminds them to be aware of their breathing so they can consciously correct it.

Proper breathing occurs when you breathe in through your nose and allow the air to fill your belly naturally first and your chest cavity second.

As you look at your bracelet throughout the day, focus on breathing through your nose instead of your mouth. It helps to pull the air into belly first so that it naturally expands. After you accomplish this phase, you'll notice that your chest naturally expands during the final quarter of your inhalation. If you focus first on your belly, the rest of the pattern will take care of itself.

Stop at least two to three times per day to count your breathing rate. A good place to shoot for is twelve to sixteen breaths per minute. As you become more fit and master your breathing, you should be able to lower your breaths per minute to six to ten. This may sound like a near-death experience given your current breaths per minute, but I assure you that your body is designed to breathe at this rate while not exercising.

Stop at least two to four times per day to count your breathing rate per minute. A good place to shoot for is twelve to sixteen breaths per minute. As you become more fit and master your breathing, you should be able to lower your breaths per minute to six to ten.

Most of us run around all day stressed out, all the while taking shallow chest breaths that stress us out even further by releasing stress hormones, such as cortisol. Again I ask the question, do you think you'll be in a positive state to change your behavior when you pile stress breathing on your already stressful day?

Posture

Think of the happiest, most confident people you know. Think about how they carry themselves. Do they walk with poise, good posture, and a brisk and confident pace appropriate for their age? The answer is likely yes. Although you may not be able to see their breathing patterns, chances are good that they're also taking deep diaphragmatic breaths that help them oxygenate their blood and their brain so they can stay sharp, alert, and vibrant.

Now let's consider posture. When you're happy, confident, and hopeful, how does your posture look? Your torso is probably erect, and your shoulders are in a neutral position (or slightly pulled back). How about when you're sad or exhausted? Chances are good that the opposite is true. Starting from the top, your head is likely down, your shoulders slumped, your torso slouched, and your lower back rounded.

If you assume such a posture, do you think your natural energy flow will be optimal? Or is this posture providing a physical environment that allows partially occluded arteries, veins, nerves, and organs? Think about it. Your body, meaning your physical body, is a literal antenna of energy. In fact, yoga is built on this premise and is designed to harness energy.

In the East, they refer to this energy as Chi, Prana, or Life Force. It's invisible and subtle in nature, and it affects the physical body in ways untold. Interestingly, researchers such as William A. Tiller have scientifically verified this subtle energy. So if you have been acculturated in the Western mind-set of "I must see it to believe it," know that science has already given its stamp of approval.

If you allow yourself to fall into bad postural patterns, you'll mitigate the natural flow of subtle energy into your body and mind and feel fatigued, sluggish, and drained. Furthermore, if you compress your spinal cord, internal organs, vessels, and joints, how can you expect your body to circulate blood, lymph, nutrients, and other life-giving fluids optimally?

Remember emotion is energy in motion, and bad posture will sap your emotions in no time flat. Furthermore, when you have bad postural patterns, you're subconsciously putting yourself into a guarded position that appears to others as defensive and self-conscious. This is hardly conducive to lifestyle change and personal development. When your posture becomes more erect and natural, you become more open to change, and you undam your natural energy conduits, putting you into a peak state that welcomes change.

To get you started in the right direction, follow these simple steps:

1. Engage in Resistance Training

Many times we develop bad posture because we allow our muscles to become weak. The muscles responsible for holding our spine in proper alignment become unable to perform their duties, leading to postural decline. This slippery slope leads to various forms of physical and mental degeneration.

Resistance training has been proven to strengthen the joints, tendons, muscles, and ligaments that are responsible for promoting optimal posture. Consider committing to a weight-training program that's specific to your needs and abilities.

2. Become Physically Aware of Your Posture

This one is simple. Your task is to become aware of your posture. I once had a client that set his watch to go off every fifteen minutes for the first three weeks of his postural realignment program. If that's not your cup of tea, employ a different method that will remind you to correct your posture.

The key here is to become aware of your posture at a conscious level. Do whatever it takes to remind yourself to correct your bad posture when needed. If you are diligent in this effort, you'll naturally start to correct your posture as your nervous system becomes aware of your new normal. Give it enough time to ensure a new physical and mental habit. This usually takes a month or two, depending on your initial postural distortion.

3. You Don't Have to Be a Soldier

Keep in mind that good posture doesn't mean that you always have to be standing at attention. In general, you want to stand straight up and let your arms hang freely at the sides. Your ears, shoulders, hips, and feet should line up. In other words, if I were to take a profile picture of you, I would be able to draw a straight line through these anatomical landmarks.

Choice of Words and Tone of Voice

If we agree that we're intelligently organized bundles of energy, and we further agree that words carry energy, it goes without saying that negative words create negative energy. The same can be said about tone of voice, so let's take it a step further, shall we?

Consider that word selection (positive or negative) and tone of voice are learned behaviors that self-replicate and thus program our subconscious mind on a daily basis. This, in turn, forms the basis of our identity at the level of our base or ego self.

Whether we like it or not, these patterns of energy form our character and personality. This is contrary to the idea that that certain personality traits are inborn and unchangeable. When we choose to live with words and tones of voice that are chronically negative, both our character and our personality become the victim of the negative energy. Given time and repetition, we become negative people.

Often those that speak negative words and utter negative tones buy into conventional wisdom. These same people utter nonsensical phrases and clichés that flow directly from their subconscious programming. When I say hello to people of this mind-set and ask them how their day is going, I often get a conditioned answer, such as "Oh, just another day in paradise" or "Another day at the rat race." Here are some other notable phrases that drain energy flow and distort reality:

- "Life is a bitch."
- "Just livin' the dream."
- "Another day, another dollar."
- "I'm doing okay for an old fart."
- "Better to be seen than to be viewed."
- "Just peachy."
- "Just taking one day at a time."

> When we choose to live with words and tones of voice
> that are chronically negative, both our character and our
> personality become the victim of the negative energy.
> Given time and repetition, we become negative people.

Keep in mind that all these and similar phrases and expressions are merely forms of excuses. They take away from our inner greatness as human beings and subjugate us to mediocrity and complacency. They essentially excuse us from our inner greatness, which guides and directs us to a higher state of being. If we had any idea how profound and powerful words and tones are, we would guard our mouth as though we were protecting our offspring from a physical threat.

To get you started in the right direction, follow these simple steps:

1. Become Aware of What's Coming Out of Your Mouth

I know this seems like a no-brainer, but we often speak as though we have no brain. In other words, we don't even think about what we're saying. We don't consider our vocabulary or think of the consequences of our choices. With this unconsciousness, we perpetuate our conditioning and lower our creative energy.

Commit to monitoring your words and tone of voice. A good way to make sure you're on track is to use your "Loving Honest Loved One" that we discussed in the goal-setting section of chapter 9. Have it serve as a feedback mechanism to hold you accountable to the words and tones that you're using. Build this into your SMART goals, and allow them to point out your slips and faults.

Don't get defensive when it corrects you. Please remember you're trying to raise your awareness. If you're reminded often of your negativity, know that it points to a problem that needs to be addressed. This exercise has the profound effect of bolstering your awareness; so in addition to your loved one, inform friends, family, and coworkers about your intentions. The more the merrier!

2. State the Opposite

Once you catch yourself using inappropriate words or tones, state the opposite on the spot. If you catch yourself saying something like "Man, I hate that I'm getting old," you can immediately replace it with "I feel alive and filled with wisdom." Keep in mind that your ego will initially defend your old thought patterns and may make you feel silly or unrealistic for uttering such positive affirmations. Just keep in mind that this will pass in time, and you'll eventually be able to do it with ease and great conviction.

3. Practice Routinely and Randomly

Remember that practice makes perfect. *Select three times out of the day that you will practice using a positive and uplifting tone of voice.* Be sure that you're alone, or practice it randomly in real-life situations. For example, let's say you see a friend in the hallway at work, and she asks you how you're doing. Instead of offering one of your normal low-energy answers as discussed above, say, "Life is good!"

Be sure to offer this expression with a smile on your face and with conviction. If you feel silly in the moment, remember that you're trying to reprogram your tired, worn-out internal dialogues and conditioned beliefs that have done nothing but drain you of your creative energy. It is time to operate from your Highest Self.

> If we had any idea how profound and powerful words
> and tones are, we would guard our mouth as though we
> were protecting our offspring from a physical threat.

Well, there we have it, my friend! You're now equipped with knowledge that will help you achieve personal power and change. In addition, these physical changes will pave the way for continued mental growth, which is the topic of our next chapter.

CHAPTER 11

EXCUSE EXORCISM 2

Mind Cop: Directing the Traffic of Your Mind through Conscious Awareness

If words are to enter men's minds and bear fruit, they must be the right words shaped cunningly to pass men's defenses and explode silently and effectually within their minds.
—J. B. Phillips

Thinking, thinking, thinking! Whether we like it or not, we can't escape it. Some of us are very good at it, and some of us are bad—very bad. The unfortunate reality is that most of us entertain chronic forms of thinking that directly detract from our wellness, happiness, and purpose.

It's estimated that the average person thinks anywhere from thirty thousand to seventy thousand thoughts per day. Now, I don't know how accurate this figure is, but I do know that whatever the number may be, the vast majority of most people's thoughts is indeed negative.

I once coached a client whom I'll call Jack, who is one of the most successful businessmen I've ever known. He has the ability to find any silver lining in any potential business deal. In business, he is an eternal optimist and usually comes out the victor.

In other areas of his life, Jack looks through a different set of lenses, which are very negative, ironically. After many deep, personal coaching sessions, I always felt a little perplexed. How could Jack be so positive in one area of his life, yet so negative in another?

When we spoke about business, he always lit up, and I could feel his positive energy. When I purposely switched the topic from business to his personal life, he also switched almost instantaneously into a negative mode, finding everything wrong with himself and with the world in general. It was as if somebody flipped a switch in his mind, resulting in a drastic perspective change.

How does this happen? I asked myself. *How can a man be so dualistic in his thinking?* I didn't found the answer until I attended a local personal development seminar where we discussed the energy of thought. Bingo! It all made sense. In that moment, I remembered reading *As a Man Thinketh* by James Allen. In that powerful book, Allen discusses how our outward world is based on our inward world of thought.

I also realized that human beings have the capacity to compartmentalize success, or lack thereof, in *multiple* areas of our lives. Have you ever known someone who is very successful in one area, say financially, but continually bombs in other areas, such as relationships or nutrition? Maybe that someone is you. This scenario applies to all of us in one way or another. In this chapter, you'll learn how to take control of the invisible force that dictates whether you will succeed or fail in *any* undertaking.

This invisible force is the force of thought. In particular, I'll discuss the ways in which you converse with yourself on a moment-to-moment basis. This is referred to as internal dialogue, and it has the power to ensure success or failure in any area of your life.

In the West, we practice an allopathic model of wellness and medicine; this means we view the body as a biomachine that can be compartmentalized into anatomical parts. With this line of thinking, it's easy to fall into the trap of separating the body and the mind. But our body and our mind make up one indivisible whole.

Most doctors subscribing to an allopathic model won't diagnose you with a thinking disorder. Nor will they recommend that you replace your negative thoughts with more empowering ones. Because of their training, most modern health care professionals don't lend credence to the enormous power of thought, especially how thought can influence your health, your well-being, and your perspective on life.

> Our body and our mind are one indivisible
> whole that is not intended to be divided.

In this chapter, you'll learn how *your body becomes a slave to your thoughts* and what you can do to master them both. It's high time that we stop subscribing to the victim mentality that states, "It's just the way that I am." If there was ever an excuse that needs to be exorcised, it's that one. So let's get after it by performing one of the most important mental exorcisms you'll ever undergo.

Exploring the Energy of Internal Dialogue

Again, everything in this world is comprised of energy, and thoughts are no exception. If you subscribe to the notion that thoughts are harmless, I have some bad yet liberating news for you: *you're wrong!*

Let's first consider this very important point: your thoughts carry an energy pattern that literally affects every cell of your body. How? Each thought carries with it an energy pattern—be it positive or negative—that influences the homeostatic balance (or health) of that cell. Thoughts are things because they are energy, just like everything else in God's universe.

> Each thought carries with it an energy pattern—
> be it positive or negative—that influences the
> homeostatic balance (or health) of that cell.

Second, we always act on what we *believe*, regardless of whether our beliefs are rooted in reality or not. Mike Wickett, in his audio book, *It's All Within Your Reach,* states,

> Whatever you believe, with feeling, becomes your reality. You are the sum total result of all your belief systems to this moment. Your beliefs form a screen of logic or a screen of prejudices through which you see the entire world. You never allow in any information that is inconsistent with your beliefs, even if you have beliefs that are totally inconsistent with reality. To the degree to which you believe these things to be true, they become true for you.[5]

To summarize, you become what you think, and what you think stems from your internal dialogue. Your internal dialogue is a 24-7 phenomenon that forms your perceptions and beliefs about reality. For example, let's pretend you foster the following internal dialogue: "I don't have time to exercise because I'm so busy at work. If I tried to exercise right now, I would end up wearing myself down and getting sick."

If you have this kind of dialogue, exercise will not be a part of your life until you *consciously* intervene and replace the dialogue with a more empowering one. Why? Because this dialogue is your truth, your standard, your value, and your inner reality. Notice I said your *inner reality* because it has nothing to do with your actual reality. It is merely a self-taught truth brought about by a *subconscious* internal dialogue.

> Your internal dialogue is a 24-7 phenomenon that forms your perceptions and beliefs about reality.

Given a chance, your internal dialogues will spread like wildfire. For example, let's say that you're enjoying your day and thinking mostly positive thoughts. All of the sudden, you get a bill in the mail that you weren't expecting, and your internal dialogue goes south in an instant.

---

[5] Mike Wickett, *It's All Within Your Reach: How to Live Your Dreams* (Nightingale-Conant Corporation, 1989).

You begin a dialogue with yourself, saying, "Man, I am sick of these stupid bills! Doesn't insurance cover anything? Why the hell do I even pay my premium? Business has been slow lately, and cash flow is low right now. Perfect! Low cash flow and high bills—not a great combination. I wish I didn't have to go through this financial strain all the time. It's just my luck!"

Have you ever been the victim of this 180-degree dialogue switch? In one moment, your internal dialogue is positive and upbeat; in the next, it's negative. This often happens to happy and positive people, and to be honest, it's okay. We all have bad days, and we all struggle with negative thoughts.

The real danger is not in having an occasional bad day, but in allowing your negative internal dialogue to go unchallenged for long periods. If allowed to persist, these dialogues can change the entire landscape and programming of your mind. Before you know it, you're seeing the world in a negative light.

This a slippery slope that can turn into a mudslide if you don't consciously intervene and replace your negative internal dialogue with something more empowering. In so doing, you will not only change your thoughts, but you will also change the accompanying energy patterns.

Directing the Traffic of Your Mind: The Gatekeeper, the Detective, and the Cop

Make no mistake; thoughts are powerful because they carry with them an energy pattern capable of programming *your subconscious mind* for better or for worst. This can be good news, or it can be very bad news. The good news is that you can use your conscious mind to elevate your awareness and reprogram your subconscious mind to run a more favorable program.

You accomplish this by acting simultaneously as the detective, the gatekeeper, and the cop of your mind. As you step into the role of mind detective, you're charged with the responsibility of finding your negative thought patterns. When you find and isolate them, you're becoming aware of them.

You'll also act as the gatekeeper of your mind. This becomes necessary when *new* thoughts arrive in your mind, which is a rarity because we tend to have the same thoughts day in and day out. As the gatekeeper, you're charged with the responsibility of allowing positive thoughts in and keeping negative thoughts out. Remember you're the gatekeeper with full authority.

I encounter this daily as a business owner as I often think about money, payroll, reinvesting, and other entrepreneurial endeavors. Every once in a while, I get sucked into a scarcity mind-set, and negative thoughts begin to enter my mind. Negative dialogues usually sound like this: "What will happen if I can't invest in my dream?" As the gatekeeper, I quickly scan this new thought and quickly label it a *nondream affirmative.* As such, it's not allowed to enter my mind.

Because the thought is negative, it now becomes my duty as the gatekeeper to *replace* it with something positive. I often replace scarcity thoughts with something like *My business is ebbing rather than flowing. I'm mature enough to know that business comes in waves. Is my business decline due to my own neglect? What am I to learn from this situation, and what (if anything) can I do about it?*

In this simple example, I was able to replace the thought rather than fight against it. Remember this age-old wisdom: that which we resist persists. The last thing you want to do is fight against your negative thoughts. Your job as the gatekeeper is to become aware of them and then replacing them.

It's important that you understand the key difference between the gatekeeper and the detective. As the gatekeeper, you're becoming aware of *new* thoughts entering your mind. As the detective, you're seeking out *old* or existing thought patterns that continually dominate your internal dialogues. Once you become aware of both old and new limiting dialogues, it's time to put on your cop hat and begin directing traffic.

Only with awareness can you accomplish the role of the cop. For years you've entertained and employed tired, worn-out dialogues that have stunted your personal and spiritual development. Compound those existing dialogues and thoughts with those currently seeking entrance into your mind, and it's easy to see why so many people become cynical.

Your duty as the cop of your mind is to direct incoming thoughts as they come and redirect existing negative ones. You accomplish this through a nonjudgmental and self-loving approach. Imagine yourself as an air-traffic controller sitting high atop a control station. You see all outgoing and incoming aircraft, so you're able to direct the planes safely and in an orderly way. In a similar fashion, you have the ability to control the traffic of your own mind through conscious awareness.

> For years you've entertained and employed
> tired, worn-out dialogues that have stunted your
> personal and spiritual development.

When you sense an old thought pattern rising to the surface, such as "I don't have time," quickly become aware of it as the detective. As the mind cop, replace it with a more empowering thought. In similar fashion, when you become aware of a *new* thought pattern coming into existence, act as the gatekeeper.

Let's pretend you're hanging around with some old friends that are spewing negative thoughts. Your gatekeeper is sleeping on the job, so some of these thoughts begin to slip into your mind. You find yourself forming a negative internal dialogue: "We live in a cruel and unfair world." Your mind cop can arrest this negative thought and replace it with a more empowering one: "The world is neutral, and I can choose to see the good or the bad. I am choosing to focus on the good."

Employing the Art of Allowing and Nonjudgment

As products of western society, most of us have been taught to believe in black and white, right and wrong, and good and evil. Though these aren't flawed or unnecessary, a black-and-white mentality often leads to labeling of others and ourselves as good or bad, right or wrong. This is particularly problematic from an energetic standpoint. Please allow me to explain.

Let's say that you have a certain value set in your mind that states that "gluttony is a sin." You've had this belief drilled into your head from childhood, and you have, for the most part, bought into it. As a general rule, you abide by this wisdom, and you don't regularly succumb to gluttony.

As you enter your midthirties, you begin to notice some weight gain in your midsection, so you decide to go on a diet that calls for less sugar. You plunge into your diet headfirst and find yourself excited for the results heading your way. Three days into your diet, you're at the home of your best friend, who is known for her legendary homemade cookies. In a moment of weakness, your internal dialogue shifts to "Oh, just one cookie won't hurt. After all, it's Friday night, and I've worked hard, so I deserve it."

As the night unfolds, you find that your one cookie has morphed into six. To drown your guilt, you decide to wash it down with a couple of beers. For the next three hours, you find yourself moping around and feeling guilty for your actions. You finally say, "Screw it! I might as well trash this whole diet thing and start over Monday."

In essence, you allowed this situation to create negative internal dialogue. Because like attracts like, your negative internal dialogue produced a negative energy field that surrounded your entire body. Metaphysical research tells us that our mental/emotional state always transcends into our physical state. In other words, when you produce negative energy through negative internal dialogues, you create a negative physical state that makes it easy to feel and act negatively.

If allowed to exist, this mental scenario will always lead to a vicious cycle of thinking that is often referred to as a rut. The good news is that you have full power to change this negative state through conscious intervention.

Let's now run the same situation using the art of *allowing and nonjudgment.* You just finished your last of the six cookies. Let's further assume that you hold a new set of conditioned beliefs: "Life is a perfect journey that teaches me what I need to learn, when I need to learn it. And it's up to me to learn it." With this mind-set, your perspective has changed for the better. Looking through this new set of lenses, you don't look at your incident as an accident, nor do you perceive yourself as a failure. You *allow* the incident to unfold, and you refuse to judge yourself.

Metaphysical research tells us that our mental/emotional state always transcends into our physical state. In other words, when you produce negative energy through negative internal dialogues, you create a negative physical state that makes it easy to feel and act negatively.

Operating from this perspective, you function from your Highest Self and see the situation as a learning opportunity. You choose to ask yourself questions like "What led me to this undesirable outcome?" or "What can I do better in the future to prepare for this kind of situation." These and other questions permeate your internal dialogue and create a positive energy that envelops your whole being. In this positive mental state, you don't host a negative internal dialogue that invites a negative energy field.

When you operate from this positive state of energy, you're able to maintain your dignity and your capacity to reason as a mature adult. You hop right back onto the wagon as though nothing happened. In truth, both of these scenarios produce energy, be it either positive or negative. The type of energy you harvest depends on your perspective and your resulting internal dialogue.

To exorcise our excuses, we must learn to live in a state of allowance and nonjudgment. In the timeless wisdom of the *Tao Te Ching*, over 2,500 years ago Lao Tzu offered us this wisdom in verse 29:

> Some think they can control what goes on.
> I don't think anyone can.
> The flow is sacred, digests
> all volition: observe it
> perturb it, try to hold it
> lose it.
> So sometimes ahead and sometimes behind,
> sometimes hot and sometimes cold,
> sometimes strong and sometimes weak,
> sometimes on top of it, sometimes under.
> So don't strain, spend too much, be smug.

In essence, there are times for weakness. These times are meant to teach us. If we approach our so-called failures with observations instead of judgments, we gain the wisdom that life is so desperately trying to teach us.

> If we desire to exorcise our excuses, we must learn to
> live in a state of allowance and nonjudgment.

When we apply the wisdom taught in the *Tao Te Ching*, we observe our behaviors and know that things happen for a reason. We also know that we're meant to experience the ups and the downs of life. The key is to see the downs as part of your perfect journey—and learn from them. This stands in stark contrast to what society teaches: we are to be perfect and not make mistakes. We are to leap into judging ourselves when we mess up. This mind-set inevitably leads us into a negative energy state.

> If we approach our so-called failures with observations
> instead of judgments, we gain the wisdom that
> life is so desperately trying to teach us.

While it may seem paradoxical when we employ this timeless wisdom, we open ourselves up to a life of joy, and we shed our excuse-making tendencies. This occurs only after we mature into a way of thinking that allows life to happen without judgment.

Summing It Up: Reconciling Your Inner Expectation through Living In the Now

At this point, you may be confused. Earlier in the book, we went over setting up a CCV (Crystal-Clear Vision) accompanied by goals. This may seem to contradict what I'm now telling you about self-judgment. How can you remain in a state of nonjudgment when you write a CCV and goals that demand self-judgment?

This can be understood through the lens of paradox. Loa Tzu had an underlying theme: it's okay to live with purpose, but it's essential to detach from the outcome. He is admonishing us to become aware of our own inner greatness so we can operate and function as our Highest Self. When we operate from this space, we innately trust that we, ourselves, are part of the all-creative Source—and therefore limitless in our potential.

With this knowledge, it's easy to live "on purpose." We detach from outcomes by not stressing out about the finish line. When we're living from our Highest Self, we have an inner knowing that we will accomplish our task, and we enjoy divine assistance. We view obstacles as learning opportunities, and failure doesn't exist. When we operate from this mind-set, there's no reason to be fixated or stressed out by an outcome. Resisting hardship or adversity ensures that we resort to a base level of thinking that's associated with base-level results.

To understand this, you must remember that you are part of the Divine—period. You may have been raised in a culture or a religion that taught you that you're a base human being entirely dependent on a higher power. I heard a sermon in which the pastor told us that we are nothing more than "filthy rags" in the sight of God and that we are utterly dependent on God for salvation.

My job is not to contend with this line of thinking; I don't wish to disrespect anybody's beliefs. My duty is to enlighten you to the fact that you're far more capable and limitless than you give yourself credit for. You are indeed part of the same source that created you.

Dr. Wayne W. Dyer, in his classic book *The Power of Intention,* states:

> You and your power of intention are not separate. So, when you form a thought within you that is commensurate with Spirit, you form a spiritual prototype that connects you to intention and sets into motion the manifestation of your desires. Whatever you wish to accomplish is an existing fact, already present in Spirit.[6]

Regardless of your religion or your spiritual beliefs, I'm sure you've had moments when you sensed this immortal truth. It's wise to extract and create your own Crystal-Clear Vision and set accompanying goals only *after* you understand that you have divinity within you. When you understand this, you'll shed any doubt that you're capable of achieving any wholesome desire of your heart.

Willpower versus Subconscious Belief

To summarize this chapter, please consider that most of your daily and habitual actions stem from your preprogrammed subconscious beliefs. We can discuss your Higher Self all day long, but if you've failed in the past to direct the traffic of your mind, you've been programmed by default to believe in lack and hardship. In short, you've been programmed to believe in your own limitations and in *reasons* for why you can't live the way you intrinsically want to live. If you fail to direct the traffic of your mind, you will by default host mental programs that can't allow your Higher Self to direct you toward your intended destination.

---

[6]   Wayne W. Dyer, PhD, *The Power of Intention: Learning to Co-create Your World Your Way* (Carlsbad, CA: Hay House, 2004).

Many people try to change their behavior through willpower alone. But even if you harness all the willpower known to humankind, you'll never change your long-term behavior, because willpower is a function of your conscious mind. If your subconscious mind is full of internal dialogues riddled with excuses, alibis, and past failures, your subconscious mind will crush your willpower, and personal development will be nothing more than a fantasy. Make no mistake; directing the traffic of your mind is a prerequisite to receiving guidance and instruction from your Higher Self.

You now have the tools that will empower you to direct the traffic of your mind and thereby further the process of reprogramming your subconscious mind. Refer back to chapter 8 for a comprehensive description of how to reprogram your subconscious mind, and then use the tips and suggestions in this chapter to reinforce the power of your Highest Self.

> Make no mistake; directing the traffic of your
> mind is a prerequisite to receiving guidance
> and instruction from your Higher Self.

Action Steps

1. Become aware of your predominating inner dialogues. What do your internal conversations look and sound like? Are they positive, and do they affirm you dream—meaning they're leading you closer to your Crystal-Clear Vision? Or are they negative and pessimistic, leading you into complacency and mediocrity?
2. Write down the *predominating themes* of your inner dialogue by actively participating in step 1. List at least five—or more if desired.
3. On a clean sheet of paper, draw a line down the middle. Label the left column "Themes" and the right "My Current Reality." Write the themes identified in step 2. For example, if you frequently host the theme "I don't have time," write it in the left-hand column.
4. On the right side, list and describe your current reality. If, for example, you use the "I don't have time" excuse often, it's practically guaranteed that your life will reflect this belief. Therefore, in the right column, labeled "My Current Reality," you would write, "I

don't make time for health and fitness." Repeat this process for each item listed in the left-hand column.

5. On a separate sheet of paper, write down a more empowering internal dialogue that will help you *replace* the self-defeating internal dialogue that you've been using for years.

6. Incorporate this into the subconscious reprogramming routine that you learned about in chapter 8.

CHAPTER 12

EXCUSE EXORCISM 3

Matrimony of Your Brain: Unify Your Left and Right Brain

A double-minded man is unstable in all his ways.
—James 1:8

In my career, I've had the privilege and honor of helping people change the way they think. Changing the way someone thinks is extremely powerful because to change someone's long-held beliefs is to change his or her life.

I'm often intrigued when I coach two people simultaneously because the results are very different, based on each individual's unique internal programming. One of my oldest clients, "Karl," is a perfect example of someone who changed his thoughts—and therefore his life.

Karl was raised to believe in conventional wisdom and in conventional practices. If he was sick, he went to the doctor without questioning a single thing. He wasn't interested in alternative or holistic remedies and believed only in conventional medical treatment.

As I began educating Karl about holistic healing approaches, his beliefs slowly began to change. He became open to the integration of conventional and holistic approaches. He solidified his beliefs as he experienced natural healing through alternative methods. Years of conventional wisdom merged with alternative approaches, and his life was enhanced as a result.

On the other end of the spectrum, countless clients scoffed at the suggestion that their ailments were, in part, related to their lifestyle choices. When I recommended homeopathic approaches or simple dietary changes, these people give me a courtesy nod while inwardly dismissing my "foolish nonsense."

I've coached hundreds of people one on one and in seminars about the power of meditation, affirmations, incantations, visualizations, and other subconscious reprogramming techniques. Most of them are initially excited about changing their lives and implementing the techniques I teach them. But I've found that only 25 to 30 percent of them make lasting lifestyle changes.

I would often get discouraged and ask myself if I was teaching flawed material or if my teaching method was missing something. I've always been genuinely intrigued by people like Karl who can quickly change their belief patterns, while others seem resistant to change and/or unable to change despite their valiant and consistent efforts.

My coaching career took a radical turn when I read the following excerpt from Karol K. Truman's enlightening book, *Feelings Buried Alive Never Die:*

> The left-brain is the thinking and the conscious side. The right brain is the feeling and the subconscious side. If we THINK in our brain that we want something in our life, but we unknowingly FEEL in our heart that we are not worthy of it, we will generally not receive it. You see—our FEELING will win, rather than our THINKING. When the two sides of the brain are not in agreement, there is inner conflict or war, and that conflict will remain in place until agreement is reached—until both sides of the brain come together.

> In order for us to experience in life what we THINK we desire, the THINKING and the FEELING have to be in unison. If the FEELING is not the same as the THINKING, then we need to change the feeling so that it becomes the same as the THINKING. After we align the THINKING and the FEELING so they are the same, we become single-minded. Until we accomplish this, we are double-minded and life works against us. When we are single-minded about what we desire in life, life works for us because, the FEELING, or heart always wins. What we FEEL is literally the "prayer of the heart," and we always receive the "prayer of our heart!"[7]

My super-successful client, Karl was actually *feeling* what I was teaching him while my other clients were only intellectually understanding what I was telling them. Could such a simple concept yield the results I was looking for as a coach? Fortunately, the answer was and is a yes. In this chapter, I'll share key concepts and principle that will help you unify your left and right brain so you can achieve the results you're seeking. This first requires a basic understanding of both brain hemispheres. It also requires that you take action directed toward the unification of them.

Understanding the Left and Right Brain

It's imperative that you understand the basic roles of your left- and right-brain hemispheres so you can unify them. Here's a partial list of the functions of the left brain:

- willpower
- linear and logical (five plus five equals ten)
- thinking
- reasoning
- analytical

---

[7]   Karol Truman, *Feelings Buried Alive Never Die* (St. George, UT: Olympus Distributing, 1991).

- expression
- formation of words
- the doer
- conscious

In contrast, consider these roles of the right brain:

- intuition
- creative
- feeling and sensing
- spiritual
- artistic
- the nurturer
- emotion/emotional
- subconscious

Note that your left brain houses the function of your conscious mind, and your right brain houses the function of your subconscious mind. Take another look at the functions of the left brain, and notice that we, as a society, live, operate, and depend primarily on left-brain function. In fact, we glorify it.

From the first day of preschool to the last day of college, we move progressively further into the domain of the left brain. Unless you studied the creative arts, chances are good that most of your education heavily involved your left brain. Society places a premium on logic and reasoning. The same can't be said about our feelings and our emotions. Such expression is typically viewed as a sign of weakness. This is particularly true in corporate America, where we're trained to act more like robots than human beings that have feelings and emotions.

To our own detriment, we're conditioned to believe that we should question our feelings and go with what "makes sense." A good example of this is how we decide what education and career to pursue. Millions of people the world over choose career paths based on the expectations of their parents and society. I've coached dozens of people who work in careers that they despise, but they continue to do so because they've *thought* their way into their career instead of respecting their *feelings*.

Our heart is designed to offer us feelings that contain infinite wisdom. These feelings guide us—when we're willing to listen to them. "Listen to your heart" is a cliché statement taught through books, music, movies, and poetry. Yet, in our modern times, few of us understand its inherent wisdom.

Your right brain is connected to your superconscious mind, or *the divine within you*. If you resonate with your superconscious mind through the *sensing of your feelings,* you'll naturally make decisions that align with your best interests. When you resonate with your superconscious mind, you live your true calling. Your true calling is what you're meant to contribute to humanity. It's the reason you exist.

I want to make it abundantly clear that I am not dogging on the left brain. As human beings, we're blessed with left-brain functions to help us navigate this earth. It's a divine gift meant to work in unison with the right brain. Problems commonly occur when we neglect this intricate balance by shifting to the domain of the left brain, and the function of the right brain is diminished.

> When you resonate with your superconscious mind, you live your true calling. Your true calling is what you're meant to contribute to humanity. It's the reason you exist.

This tends to happen when norms are established. Conditioned norms come in all shapes and sizes, be they religious, political, medical, or cultural. Many established norms lead to inauthenticity. Ironically, the right brain digs us out of trouble and helps us to advance personally and as a society.

To illustrate my point, let's turn to the issue of slavery. If we could see into the mind-set of slave owners, we would find that left-brained thinking dominates. Thoughts such as "they are my property and therefore subject to my desires" were common and condoned by society. Politicians often ran their campaigns on pro-slavery tickets and appealed to the "logic" that millions of people shared at that time.

Ironically, yet inevitably, what ended slavery were the *intuition and feelings* that exist in our collective superconscious right brain. Keep in mind that our superconscious mind is our direct connection to our Higher Self or God. Famous authors such as Napoleon Hill have often referred to this connection as infinite intelligence. This infinite intelligence, coupled with our logical left brain, is solely responsible for all human progress, innovation, and good. There's a simple reason for this: any wisdom gleaned from our right brain comes directly from the "God within us" or our Higher Self.

When we dismiss our right brain and rely solely on our left brain, we experience corruption and moral decay. Slavery ended because of people like Abraham Lincoln, who were not afraid or ashamed to use their right-brain function. If we look back at any historical advancement, such as women's suffrage or the end of segregation, we clearly see the right-brain function at work.

> Slavery ultimately ended because of people like
> Abraham Lincoln, who were not afraid or ashamed to
> become unified with their right-brain function.

No human advancement has ever happened without our collective right brain becoming our dominant and default mode of thinking. Only when we begin to *feel* with our right brain collectively does real societal change happen.

Leading up to the abolition of slavery, the left brain was dominant because it crowded out any feeling from the right brain. When a slave owner heard a slight whispering from his soul, he quickly dismissed it with the logic of his left brain. He pointed to the proofs of every other slave owner and thereby felt justified. He then reasoned, "Everybody else is doing it, so it is normal. I am justified."

When we finally began to *feel* what our hearts were telling us, we stopped for a moment of reflection. We began to feel in our heart and through our right brain. When we looked into the eyes of a slave, we see a living, breathing, and loving human being—and we *felt* for that person. We subsequently realized that what we had been doing for hundreds of years was wrong. It forced us to reject the logic and rationalization of our overly active left brain.

The term *progressivism* could easily be a synonym for the unification of the left and right side of the brain. Any form of human progress stems from their matrimony or unification—period. Inventors consistently rely on the creative faculty of their right brain, or superconscious mind, to harness information that was previously unavailable to humankind.

Albert Einstein, Thomas Edison, and other geniuses all tapped into a source of knowledge previously unknown through a full allowance of their right-brain function. Remember—your right brain connects you to your subconscious and superconscious mind, which is the mind of God.

> The term progressivism could easily be a synonym for the unification of the left and right side of the brain. Any form of human progress stems from their matrimony or unification—period.

These insightful people were able to synthesize left- and right-brain functions. In other words, they respected the balance and power of their left and right brains. As a result of this left-right brain balance, we are the fortunate recipients of these geniuses' advancements.

Exorcising Your Excuses by Unifying Your Brain

If the unification of our collective mind worked to end slavery and aid in the societal advancements that we now enjoy, can it also help you in your individual life? Can it help you exorcise your excuses and obtain the life of your dreams? Without a doubt, the answer is and always will be a resounding *yes*.

Are you a frustrated personal-development junkie? Have you stated affirmations for years, meditated for decades, and vividly visualized your dream life but haven't yet realized it? If the answer is yes, it's likely that you've also defined your dream, intellectualized it, visualized it, and acted as if it were already a reality. Yet you still see no change, and you continue to live the life that you want so desperately to change.

If you connect with this description, your left brain and your right brain haven't been properly unified. The problem is that you have left-brained yourself to death. People who are workhorses by nature set a goal, get fired up about it, work hard, and use their left brain to obtain their goal, yet they come up empty-handed every time.

Only when you *feel* your intended reality will it become your reality.

Let's say, for example, that you've set a financial goal. You want to make a six-figure income, so you write out your CCV and your goals for making it happen. You even write out a list of affirmations (see chapter 8). You faithfully read your CCV and goals every day and night. Day after day, you wait with your fingers crossed to see your dream life come true—only to up come with nothing. What could be more frustrating? Why is this happening?

Here's why: You used every facet, searched every nook and cranny, and exploited all your left-brain capacity. You used willpower, employed logic, wore out common sense, and used up every other aspect of your left brain. You were very conscious but not superconscious. You *thought* with your left brain, but you didn't *feel* with your right brain. You had a conscious vision of what you wanted, but your subconscious programming didn't agree with what you were consciously telling yourself.

In short, your feelings didn't match your vision. Therefore, *you didn't believe yourself at a subconscious level.* Without your right brain, or subconscious, on board, nothing—I repeat, *nothing*—will ever change in your life. Why? Because if your subconscious mind is running a conditioned program that's contrary to your dream, and if you remain unaware of it, you're unlikely to tap into the power of your right brain.

Only through the use of your right brain do you connect to your superconscious mind, or your Higher Self. You must unify your subconscious, your conscious, and your superconscious minds. You accomplish this through the unification of your left and right brain. I know these are bold and often sobering facts, but as the old saying goes, "The devil you don't know is more dangerous than the devil you do know."

To make sure you don't spiral into depression, let's work on getting your left and right brain together. Let's get them flirting and engaged so they will come together in holy matrimony. The following steps are a supplement to what you learned in chapters 4 and 8. These steps are laser-focused to help you unify your brain and get the results that have previously eluded you.

A Step-by-Step Guide to Unifying Your Brain

Step 1: Smile

This may sound like the most absurd suggestions yet, but consider that many experts, such as Mark Stibich of Columbia University, have demonstrated multiple benefits of smiling, ranging from lowering blood pressure to less stress. Other researches, such as J. D. Laird[8] and F. Strack,[9] have manipulated subjects' facial expressions manually or had them hold a pencil in their mouths while watching cartoons. The subjects found the cartoons funnier when they were forced to smile.

If smiling can lower your blood pressure, relieve your stress, change your mood for the better, and give you a better outlook on life, wouldn't it stand to reason that it can help you feel and sense your goals and dreams? Of course it does because it brings animation into your life. This is why I ask you to do the following:

---

[8]   J. D. Laird, "Self-attribution of emotion: the effects of expressive behavior on the quality of emotional experience," *Journal of Personality and Social Psychology* 29, no. 4 (April 1974): 475–86.

[9]   F. Strack, L.L. Martin, and S. Stepper, "Inhibiting and facilitating conditions of the human smile: a nonobtrusive test of the facial feedback hypothesis," *Journal of Personality and Social Psychology* 54, no. 5 (May 1988): 768–77.

- Smile. Yes, smile when you're reading your CCV, as presented in chapter 8. Do the same when you're stating affirmations, as indicated in chapter 4.

- Smile for the hell of it! Why not? When you're walking down the street, smile at those who pass you by, and offer them a friendly hello. You don't have to be phony. Just offer a sincere smile because you're alive and have everything to be grateful for. You might even find that you enjoy doing this.

- Smile at yourself when you "mess up," especially if you tend to beat yourself up and spiral into negative internal dialogues. By smiling, you stay positive and invite feelings conducive to the unification or your left and right brain.

- When moments of anger and frustration come, smile about them *immediately* afterward. You'll have your "moments," and that's fine. You're a human being, so you're meant to experience a myriad of emotions. As I stated earlier, the problem is when you allow yourself to stay there. Smiling and even laughing at yourself can change your mood and get you back into a positive state of mind. Remember positivity is the only state of mind that allows optimal right-brain function.

Constantly remind yourself that you're trying to recalibrate and reprogram your subconscious mind so that it will align with your left-brain thinking. You can never logically think your way into an emotion, so why not help yourself along by smiling and *creating* the emotion? The good news is that your subconscious mind can't tell the different between a forced smile and a real one. That said, get to the point where smiling is natural, real, and pleasurable for you. This can be mastered only through intentional repetition of the steps above.

Step 2: Leave Judgment Homeless

We live in a world of judgment. We judge ourselves, we judge others, we judge right and wrong, and we judge just about everything else. While certain forms of judgment are necessary for our well-being and safety, the judgment I speak of is inappropriate judgment of yourself and others.

Judgment typically comes from rules—*your* rules. We have all rules within us that we've been conditioned to believe in. These rules involve our career, money, relationships, justice, morality, ethics, religion, and more.

While rules aren't bad, judgment stems from rules. Think about it. If you have set a rule about a particular parenting style, you've subconsciously bought into the notion that your form of parenting is right. By doing this, you also set up boundaries and parameters for yourself—a certain code of ethics, if you will. This is not a problem, because human beings are guaranteed to have a varied set of rules, though there are no two people that share the same rulebook.

Years ago, I was training a client who asked in a stern voice if he could have a moment of my time. "Of course," I said, and into my office we went. He closed my office door behind him and proceeded to berate me over my business practices and my "lack of caring." He told me that if I didn't live up to his elaborate standards, which took him thirty minutes to explain on my whiteboard, my business was doomed to fail.

As I look back at this experience, I chuckle because I can see all too clearly what happened. I had violated this man's "rules of business." He was a high-powered, buttoned-down attorney and extremely stoic. Keep in mind that this client received everything and more that he expected from my services. He lost weight, was eating impeccably, and gained a lifestyle that he was very proud of. In fact, his baggy T-shirt morphed into a baggy tank top, which then morphed into a very tight tank top. He obviously got what he paid for, but he couldn't let go of the fact that I didn't run my business the way he wanted it run. *His rules were violated.*

The point here is very simple. When we set rules for ourselves, we often subconsciously project them onto others. We expect them to live by our rules, and when they don't, we find ourselves getting upset, agitated, and even pissed off. When laboring under these types of feelings, it's 100 percent impossible to unify our left and right brain for one simple reason: the energy they produce is negative and of a very low vibration. How can we create anything positive when we're wallowing in a negative energy field akin to quicksand?

> We expect them to live by our rules, and when they don't, we find ourselves getting upset, agitated, and even pissed off.

The solution is simple. First, you must clearly define what your rules are. If you find that you have rules that no longer serve you, get them the hell out of your head and/or replace them. As I've discussed, having rules can be a good thing if you have clearly defined them and they truly serve you—that is, they create a reasonable standard of living that brings fulfillment and joy into your life. Likewise, they're hindering you if they put undo pressure on you or cause anxiety and stress.

Second, make sure you don't set too many rules for yourself or others. Simplify your rules so you don't find yourself inundated or confounded by unnecessary ones. Your inner wisdom will tell you which rules are appropriate and which need to be deleted from your brain.

Be sure you clearly define your rules in your relationships. This is only fair to people you are in a relationship with. If you aren't clear, you're demanding that they comply with your rules without even knowing them. The last time I checked, mind reading was reserved to psychics.

Third, make sure your rules bring you joy. Set them so that they empower you and allow you to live the life you deserve. One of my personal rules is that I treat all people I come in contact with the same, regardless of their social status. Whether I coach a CEO of a corporation or a janitor, I treat them the same. Both are deserving of my respect and my Highest Self.

In the past, I set rules that have ultimately brought me pain and suffering, and I was forced to abandon them. I say *forced* because they were my rules and my rules only. Nobody forced me to set those rules, but my Higher Self forced me to abandon them. When you create a rule, it temporarily becomes part of who you are. This is the bad news. The good news is that you can unlearn unnecessary and harmful rules using the guidelines you are now learning.

Step 3: Forgive Yourself and Others, and Love Unconditionally

So setting too many rules can lead to the judgment of others and oneself. And we can't operate from our Highest Self under those conditions. The following sequence of logic will help you understand why this is the case:

- Regardless of your spiritual or religious beliefs, you believe that you came from a source of unconditional love.
- Your connection to this source is your superconscious mind—or the mind of God—meaning that you can commune with and know God's will through this source. It's interesting to note that all major world religions teach this in one form or another. For the record, it doesn't matter who or what you believe God to be; it only matters that this source is unconditional love.
- Your source of creation creates *everything* (including you) through unconditional love. This may sound confusing at first glance, and I won't try to explain it here; consider researching it further.
- Unconditional love is an energy that vibrates at a super-high frequency and is currently undetectable through instruments.
- Lower forms of energy that emanate from the judgment of self and others do *not* resonate with the energy of unconditional love. In fact, when you're living in these lower energy patterns, it takes away from your spiritual nature and leads you to believe in all the labels and notions that judgment creates. Any time you engage in negative thinking, such as, "I lack willpower," it directly contradicts the divine energy pattern that stems from the source of unconditional love.
- When you live from a place of unconditional love, you're concomitantly resonating with the energy that emanates from your Highest Self or the Divine within you. Under these conditions, you're directly connected to your spiritual source.
- When you're connected to your spiritual source, you become capable of *creation*. You're able to create your innermost desires,

dreams, and drive that stem from your Higher Self. In this state, you'll never have to wonder if you're fulfilling your true calling, because your Higher Self reveals that knowledge to you.

- Remember that your superconscious mind operates and functions predominantly through your right brain—not your left.
- If you remain in a state of judgment, it's impossible to stay connected to your source, because you remain trapped in your left brain.

Here is the bottom line: Without the use and function of your right brain, you remain divided and unable to manifest the deepest and most powerful desires of your heart. In this state, you stunt yourself spiritually. When you do that, you automatically stunt yourself emotionally, mentally, physically, intellectually, and socially. So you set yourself up for excuse making because your ego, which operates in your left brain, becomes obsessed with defending all the false labels that it has created for you.

Without the use and function of your right brain, you remain divided … When you do that, you automatically stunt yourself emotionally, mentally, physically, intellectually, and socially. So you set yourself up for excuse making because your ego, which operates in your left brain, becomes obsessed with defending all the false labels that it has created for you.

Let's talk about how to remedy the disastrous consequences of judgment. This magic elixir comes down to one of the most powerful roles of the human heart: *forgiveness*. When I speak of forgiveness, I speak of *unconditional forgiveness* for yourself and others. When either I or someone else has treated me poorly, I used to convince myself that I had truly forgiven myself or my offender.

But, true to my ego, I often find hidden emotions surfacing when I or my offender makes the mistake that warranted forgiveness in the first place. I feel the same feelings that existed previous to my so-called forgiveness. In these circumstances, my soul teaches me that I haven't truly forgiven others or myself.

Judgment stems from broken rules that we hold ourselves or others to. Again, it's okay to have rules for ourselves, but we must be willing to forgive ourselves when we break them. This takes a lot of practice and a high degree of spiritual maturity, but it gets easier with practice.

When you view life as a journey that teaches you through your mistakes, it becomes effortless and natural to forgive yourself. On the other hand, if you create a million rules for yourself and a black/white, right/wrong mentality, it becomes impossible not to judge yourself or others.

Be willing to look at life as a perfect journey that teaches perfectly. Resist the urge to categorize yourself and others based on your rules. Be willing to look into the eyes of other human beings and know that they come from the same source of unconditional love that created you. Resist the urge to correct other human beings and demand that they live by your rules. Realize that they are on their own perfect journey and are being taught on their own divine timetable.

In short, drop the judgment and forgive yourself and others unconditionally. If people have offended you, forgive them unconditionally. Call them up this moment (if appropriate), and offer your unconditional love and forgiveness. If you find this hard to do, rest assured that your ego is playing hardball. It's defending all the reasons that they're wrong and illustrating how you're right.

> Be willing to look at life as a perfect journey that teaches perfectly. Resist the urge to categorize yourself and others based on your rules. Be willing to look into the eyes of other human beings and know that they come from the same source of unconditional love that created you.

If you truly desire to unify your left and right brain, don't let your ego dominate your thinking. Once your ego takes charge, you become incapable of communing with your Higher Self or the Divine within you. Instead, you remain subservient to your ego, needing to be right at all costs.

Though it isn't an easy task, but you *must* forgive anybody that is causing you ill feelings. If you doubt your ability to forgive, know that forgiveness of yourself and others is possible if you truly *desire* it. Truly forgiving yourself and others is, without question, one of the most spiritually liberating activities in this mortal life. From unconditional forgiveness comes unconditional love. From unconditional love comes your Highest Self, a place where excuses can't exist.

> Truly forgiving yourself or others is without question one
> of the most spiritually liberating activities that can be
> experienced in this mortal life. From unconditional forgiveness
> comes unconditional love. From unconditional love comes
> your Highest Self, a place where excuses can't exist.

Step 4: Uncover and Dismiss Hidden Emotions

Through Karol K. Truman's *Feelings Buried Alive Never Die*, I learned about the true power of emotions and feelings and how they impact our physical, mental, emotional, and spiritual health. Feelings carry with them a certain energy pattern that never leaves your body unless you become aware of them and dismiss them.

The dismissal of these emotions and feelings is accomplished through a spiritual practice that Truman guides you through in her book. I won't try to elaborate or embellish on anything that comes from her masterpiece, as I don't want to do a disservice to her work.

For this step, purchase and read her book so you can uncover feelings that are affecting your life and bolstering your proclivity to make excuses. The book is a quick read and very easy to apply. It's a life changer and a prerequisite for exorcising your excuses.

Step 5: Nurturing Your Right Brain through Affirmations

Let's do a nonscientific experiment. Talk to fifteen people today, and ask them if they work on reprogramming their subconscious mind through repeated daily affirmations. I guarantee that you'll receive cockeyed looks. Your friends and peers might think you've lost your mind. It's unfortunate that affirmations are still considered a fringe practice when they have been scientifically documented to reprogram the subconscious mind.

In chapters 4 and 8, you were educated as to affirmations' value and how to properly perform them. In this step, I give you some affirmations based on some of the excuses I hear the most. Keep in mind that the following affirmations are only examples and are meant to help you construct your own affirmations based on your conditioned beliefs and/or excuses.

Excuse: "I don't have time to exercise."[10]

Affirmation: "Exercise is a top priority for me, and I make time for it daily."

Excuse: "I can't afford it."

Affirmation: "I come from a place of abundance that provides for my needs."

Excuse: "I'm too tired for exercise."

Affirmation: "Appropriate exercise gives me energy and helps me sleep better."

Excuse: "I am too old for _____" (fill in the blank).

Affirmation: "I feel young and capable of doing anything that I set my mind to."

Excuse: "I don't have any interest in changing _____" (fill in the blank with anything that would help you grow).

Affirmation: "I am worth the effort of personal change."

---

[10] Keep in mind that the time excuse is the most common excuse in the world. Find the areas in your life that are affected by this nasty little excuse.

Excuse: "I'm lazy."

Affirmation: "I'm passionate about life and eager to better myself."

Excuse: "I don't know how."

Affirmation: "The answers I seek exist through other people, services, technology, and my own soul."

Excuse: "It's too hard."

Affirmation: "I embrace challenge, and I revel in the rewards it brings."

Excuse: "I'm not smart enough."

Affirmation: "I come from an all-knowing Source of unconditional love, and I'm part of that Source. I'm therefore a brilliant and capable being."

Excuse: "Nobody will support me in my efforts."

Affirmation: "I always incur the favor of those who are meant to help and serve me."

Excuse: "Healthy food is gross."

Affirmation: "Healthy food nourishes my body, and I find it delicious."

Excuse: "Healthy food is too expensive."

Affirmation: "I never put a price on my health. My body is worthy of premium-grade fuel."

Excuse: "I don't have time to prepare healthy food or meals."

Affirmation: "I make time for healthy food prep, and I find it enjoyable."

Excuse: "My spouse/significant other makes it difficult for me to change."

Affirmation: "I'm a proactive individual and forge my own destiny without excuses."

Excuse: "I'm too busy to change at this point in my life. I'll have to wait for a more reasonable time to change."

Affirmation: "I'm fully capable of changing in the instant of my desire."

Excuse: "I have failed too many times in the past to succeed now."

Affirmation: "The past has no bearing on my present or future. I live in the now and therefore determine my own destiny."

Excuse: "I am not loved."

Affirmation: "I come from a place of unconditional love, and I exude unconditional love."

Excuse: "I have incurred God's disfavor/wrath."

Affirmation: "I came from a source of unconditional love that supports me in all my dreams and aspirations."

Affirmation: "I operate from unconditional love and refrain from dogmatic practices."

Excuse: "My family and friends don't support my change."

Affirmation: "I love everybody unconditionally and expect nothing in return."

Excuse: "I have low self-esteem"

Affirmation: "I am worthy of self-love"

Excuse: "I'm a failure."

Affirmation: "I never fail. I only learn."

Excuse: "I will look stupid if I fail" or "I fear criticism."

Affirmation: "What other people think of me is none of my business"

Excuse: "I will never reach my potential."

Affirmation: "I'm guided by my Higher Self to my divine potential."

Excuse: "I am not capable."

Affirmation: "I can accomplish anything my heart desires."

Excuse: "I'm stressed out."

Affirmation: "I live in the present and deal with one thing at a time. Life by the inch is a cinch."

Affirmation: "I choose to enjoy the good, the bad, and the ugly; it is all part of my perfect journey."

Excuse: "What if I don't live up to the expectations of others or of society?"

Affirmation: "I live my own life and follow the divine and ethical desires of my heart."

Excuse: "I don't possess the confidence to succeed."

Affirmation: "I exude confidence. I live confidence. I *am* confidence!"

These are just a few of the limitless excuses we tend to make. Be honest with yourself, and find the internal dialogues and excuses that pervade your thinking. Be kind and gentle with yourself, and realize that we *all* foster excuses to one degree or another. Therefore, there's no reason to feel guilt or shame for having them.

If you find yourself feeling silly or embarrassed while uttering your affirmations, just remind yourself that you're trying to reprogram your subconscious mind, which is currently filled with silly excuses. If you look at it from this logical perspective, you'll have no logical reason to feel silly or embarrassed for participating in this very powerful and life-changing practice.

> If you find yourself feeling silly or embarrassed while uttering your affirmations, just remind yourself that you're trying to reprogram your subconscious mind, which is currently filled with silly excuses.

Step 6: Eat Well to Feel Well

I'll cover this topic extensively in the next chapter. Suffice it to say that without good nutrition, you can *try* to think well, exercise well, and meditate until you levitate; but when it comes down to reality, you can only feel well after your body is properly nourished. In the next chapter, you'll learn the profound impact nutrition has on your psychology.

Step 7: Sleep Well to Feel Well

I'll cover this extensively in chapter 14. Suffice it to say that without good sleep, it becomes impossible to unify your left and right brain for many physiological and psychological reasons. For now, be sure to get at least eight hours of sleep per night, and make any changes necessary to employ this healthful and necessary practice.

Step 8: Wiggle Out of Negativity

Wiggle is my cute way of saying *exercise.* I will cover this extensively in chapter 15. Suffice it to say that you'll always move yourself out of a negative mind-set faster than you can talk yourself out of it. This is why it's wise to state your affirmations while walking, jogging, or moving briskly. For now, be sure that you're exercising at least five times per week and staying as active as possible.

Step 9: Invite Creativity, Abstraction, and Gray into Your Life

Again, your left brain functions in the realm of logic and linear reason while your right brain enjoys abstraction, creativity, and spirituality. With this in mind, it's wise to step out of your ridged left-brained routine and experience the thrill of your right brain. To do this, try some to these simple suggestions:

- Bust out of your normal routine. If you're used to going on a morning walk, consider going for a swim or meditating instead. Mix it up!
- Observe nature, and notice how your left brain tries to make sense of everything. It's as though it's trying to make a logical pattern out of nature when one doesn't exist. Become aware of this tendency, and allow your eyes to take in only "what is." Allow nature to exist without trying to make logical sense of it. Ironically, Mother Nature uses her apparent chaos to form a perfect harmony that sustains all life. Be present with this chaos, and allow your mind to take it in without judgment or need to correct.
- Try art, even if you are not artistic. Leave your ego at the door, and detach from the outcome. Allow your mind to draw whatever feels right. Be aware of the tendency of your left brain to take over to make sure that everything is drawn "just right." Instead, allow your abstract nature to take over.
- Entertain a different point of view. This can be hard, but give it a try. If you're a Christian, thoughtfully consider what a Jewish person believes—and vice versa if you're Jewish. If you're politically conservative, consider entertaining a more liberal viewpoint. You don't have to adopt these views; just open your mind to them so you can balance your left and right brain.

Well, there you have it, my friend. I know it has been a long chapter, and I thank you for sticking with me. The application of the principles discussed within this chapter will revolutionize your life and allow you to exorcise your excuses.

CHAPTER 13

EXCUSE EXORCISM 4

Nutri-Lizing Your Excuses

Exorcise Your Excuses through the Power of Natural Nutrition

Let food be thy medicine and medicine be thy food.
—Hippocrates

As a level 3 CHEK Holistic Lifestyle coach, I work with many wonderful people to help them discover just how powerful nutrition can be in their lives. Witnessing nutritional change in someone's life is one of my greatest blessings. Conversely, I'm cursed with an abundant and ever-growing library of nutritional knowledge that allows me to see the world in a different way than the general public. Please allow me to explain.

As I work with clients of all shapes and sizes, I see many who are suffering from disease, obesity, body-image crises, and a wide variety of ailments ranging from indigestion to cancer. Most of them have been to doctors and therapists, and have tried many quick fixes. While they may experience temporary relief with these approaches, they ultimately find themselves back where they started. Many of these people have convinced themselves that they're getting older, so their aches, pains, low energy, and weight gain are normal. Yet they find themselves in my office looking for solutions.

In a study from 2002 to 2009, the Centers for Disease Prevention and Control stated that approximately 70 percent of deaths in the United States and 75 percent of total health care costs are attributable to chronic disease.[11] The diseases topping the chart are

- cardiovascular disease,
- cancer,
- chronic lower respiratory disease,
- cerebrovascular disease, and
- diabetes.

Most people seem to view obesity and disease rates as inevitable. We look at the climbing diabetes and cancer rates and say, "These facts are unfortunate. I hope science will catch up to this sooner rather than later." Such thoughts absolve us of responsibility. When something goes wrong with our health, we run to doctors and expect them to fix us. Preventive living is an afterthought in our fast-paced world.

When I'm working in a corporate environment, I see most of the employees eating fast food, vending machine food, and processed food. In short, they're eating food that can be prepared and eaten within five or ten minutes. They run to their meetings while forgetting to drink water, claiming that water is boring or gross. I find it ironic that these same people never forget to drink coffee or their favorite soda to keep them going.

When I pick up my kids from school, I watch as other kids opening their lunch boxes. I see only boxed juices, chips, dried fruit, and the so-called healthy Lunchable. Fast-forward to my girls' soccer games. Never a game goes by that doesn't conclude with a sugary treat for a job well done. As I drive home, I see billboards for McDonald's, Arby's, Sonic, and other restaurants tempting their customers with close-ups of their burgers, fries, and milkshakes. It seems that I can't go anywhere without living in the world of junk food.

---

[11] Centers for Disease Control and Prevention, Chronic Disease Overview, accessed on October 31, 2008.

It's estimated that up to 90 percent of all disease comes from poor lifestyle choices, diet being chief among them. So, what does all this have to do with exorcising your excuses?

Would you believe me if I told you that your food affects every cell in your body? Would you believe that it affects your brain, your nervous system, your endocrine system, and every other system and organ?

Unhealthy eating affects your mood, your thoughts, your intellect, your hormones, your perceptions, and your energy levels. It creates an internal physiological environment that's conducive to making poor choices. Taken one step further, and you see that poor choices leading to excuse making. Let's dive in and find out how.

You Are What You Eat: Establishing the Link between Your Diet and Your Behavior

"You are what you eat!" We've all heard this statement, but few of us consider how literal it is. Most of us don't look at a Coke or a Twizzler that we are about to pound down and say to ourselves, *Well, I'd better pass, because I know that this is going to be part of my body.*

Instead, we make an excuse, justify why we deserve it, and proceed to block out any harmful consequences that might be caused by our nutritional decision. Even if we entertain the thought that our poor choices add inches to our waistline, we rarely entertain the thought that these foods become the building blocks of our body down to the cellular level.

Our decision to consume junk food might not be as easy if we take the time to consider that it takes matter to build matter. In other words, the food you eat is the matter that builds your very cells. The doughnut you ate yesterday becomes the building blocks for your blood, lymphatic fluids, bones, and organs. The highly processed TV dinner you made last night is now making a new home in your eyeballs, knees, or throat. The hot dog you ate one week back has now been broken down, digested, and recomposed into your heart and liver tissue.

> Even if we entertain the thought that our poor choices
> add inches to our waistline, we rarely entertain
> the thought that these foods become the building
> blocks of our body down to the cellular level.

Many experts have told us that the human body completely regenerates itself in one year. This means every cell that constitutes your physical body will no longer be a part it come one year from now. In other words, the food that you eat is processed and metabolized by your body and, in turn, *becomes your body*. It's a physiological fact that your hormones, neurotransmitters, nerves, and every cell of your being is composed of what you eat.

> It's a physiological fact that your hormones, neurotransmitters,
> nerves, and every cell of your being is composed of what you eat.

Let's take a look at one of my personal case studies. Her name was Jamie, and I affectionately nicknamed her Jamie the Junk-Food Junkie. She was a superstar player for the typical American diet—a busy woman who was always on the run. She found herself running to quick sugary snacks and processed foods that required little preparation. Her diet was low in fat because she was socially conditioned to believe in the "evil" of fat.

Jamie was notorious for mood swings. Often she would enter my office with a load of energy and enthusiasm. Other times, I found her to be challenging, emotional, condescending, and riddled with excuses for not progressing in her nutritional plan. Interestingly, I could almost always link her emotional swings to what she ate during the previous twenty-four hours. Let's dive into the science of why Jamie faced emotional challenges.

First, sugar. Jamie would take in about one hundred grams of sugar per day, and the number of grams would steadily increase proportionate to her stress levels. Sugar is an acidic substance, and it has the potential to disturb the delicate acid-to-alkaline ratio in your body. When acid starts to predominate in the body, the body typically starts to crave more alkaline foods, such as leafy greens and other alkaline rich foods—unless you're addicted to sugar, as was Jamie.

Because Jamie was so addicted to sugar, her brain interpreted any craving for real food as a craving for sugar. This started a vicious cycle that left her with cravings and feelings of constant hunger. The question is this: Do you think that this physiological state is conducive to a good psychological state? What is the likelihood of Jamie making good decisions when her body is at war with the acid bath within her arteries, veins, and cells? Is it any wonder that she becomes spacy and irritable when her diet is off-kilter?

Now let's take a look at what sugar did to Jamie's nervous system. The nervous system is one of the most intelligent and intuitive systems in the body. It's comprised of the brain, the spinal cord, and all the nerves that feed the entire human body. At a rudimentary level, it's set up to help you accomplish two very important objectives:

- Seek pleasure.
- Avoid pain.

If you study human evolution up to our present day, you find this truth: our nervous system is designed to protect us from danger, and it aids us in seeking pleasure in all its forms. Left unadulterated by poor food choices and other negative lifestyle choices, our nervous system helps us make wise choices. It works closely with our intuition as we navigate this earthly plane.

There are two main branches to the nervous system: the autonomic nervous system and the somatic nervous system. The somatic nervous system heeds your consciousness. In other words, when you want to move your muscles, it allows your conscious intention to be translated into physical motion. Simple enough.

Left unadulterated by poor food choices and other negative lifestyle choices, our nervous system helps us make wise choices. It works closely with our intuition as we navigate this earthly plane.

The autonomic nervous system makes life a lot easier because you don't have to think about all the actions it constantly performs. It makes your heart beat, circulates your blood and your lymphatic fluids, and attends to thousands of biochemical reactions that allow you to stay upright and living.

The autonomic nervous system is further broken down into two units. The first is the sympathetic nervous system, which—without going into too much detail—is designed to help you *go, go, go*. It's your green light. It helps you accomplish your daily tasks by orchestrating essential physiological steps that *liberate energy* into your body and thus allow movement.

The liberation of energy is a catabolic process—that is, a physiological process that breaks down molecules into smaller units that are either oxidized to release energy or used to build up other energetic compounds. For example, when you need energy because you're low on food, your body catabolically releases glucose (or stored sugar) from your liver in a process known as gluconeogenesis.

The second unit of your nervous system is the parasympathetic. It tells you to *slow down*. It's your red light. It helps you to recoup and recover from the catabolic actions of your sympathetic nervous system by orchestrating physiological steps that help to accumulate (rather than liberate) energy in your body. Think of this branch of the nervous system as the hoarder of energy, while the sympathetic branch is the "exploiter" of energy. The parasympathetic hoarding of energy eventually leads to the liberation or usage of energy by the sympathetic nervous system.

Both of these branches are essential for living a balanced and healthy life that doesn't lead to burnout—or worse, disease. They're meant to keep each other in check so we remain physiologically balanced. When imbalance occurs, it does so on the sympathetic side.

Sadly, we live in a fast-paced society that keeps our sympathetic nervous system engaged and revving in the red zone far beyond what is healthy for the human body.

Now let's get back to Jamie and see how her dietary habits contributed to her emotional imbalances and excuse making. Sugar is a known sympathetic nervous system stimulant. It stimulates the sympathetic nervous system by revving it up. This is why millions of Americans turn to coffee and sugar regularly. They depend on these substances to stimulate their sympathetic nervous system so they can make it through the day.

> We live in a fast-paced society that keeps our sympathetic nervous system engaged and revving in the red zone far beyond what is healthy for the human body.

If our physiology is balanced, we don't have to turn to addictive substances (yes, sugar is an addictive substance) to stimulate our sympathetic nervous system. Under normal nutritional circumstances, the nervous system remains in a state of balance. It should be able to fend for itself without chemical assistance generated by sugar and/or caffeine.

Here's what happened internally when Jamie continually turned to sugar and junk food: Her sympathetic nervous system was essentially forced into a fight-or-flight response, even though she wasn't facing a life-threating situation. Her dietary sugar became a form of stress to her body. Whenever this happened, her HPA axis (involving the hypothalamus and the pituitary and adrenal glands) was activated, and the adrenal glands released two primary stress hormones: adrenaline and cortisol. These hormones aid in the catabolic liberation of energy from the liver and muscles.

As you might imagine, this is not a normal physiologic response. Although sugar from any source (be it natural or refined) stimulates the nervous system, sugars from natural sources are accompanied by nutrients that help regulate and normalize the nervous system response. When you eat highly processed sugar, which is found in nearly all foods, imbalances begin to occur.

When you repeatedly introduce cortisol into your body, it brings with it a plethora of undesirable consequences, including the following:

- mood swings
- irritably
- anxiousness
- food cravings
- muscle tension
- joint tension
- hormonal imbalance
- inability to concentrate
- poor decision making

Keep in mind that these symptoms are only the tip of the iceberg, but just know this: when your cortisol is high, it makes you cranky, anxious, and unclear in your thinking.

> When your cortisol is high, it makes you cranky,
> anxious, and unclear in your thinking.

Here's a simple question: Do you think it's possible to make rational, well-thought-out decisions when you're cranky, anxious, irritable, and unclear in your thinking? No. And that's why Jamie experienced unpredictable mood swings. She had essentially created an internal hormonal environment that was so far off normal that she was pitting her intentions of personal development against her internal biochemistry. The bad news for Jamie and possibly for you can be summed up in this very important truth: you can *never* think, meditate, pray, or Zen yourself into a place of tranquility when your physiology is at war with itself.

> You can never think, meditate, pray, or Zen yourself into a
> place of tranquility when your physiology is at war with itself.

When clients want to change their lifestyles, I often start with their diet—*not* their mind. That's because our physiology profoundly affects our psychology. In fact, your physiology is the ground substance for your psychology. If your physiology is being interrupted or thrown off by bad nutritional choices, it then becomes *impossible* to elevate your state of mind. Jamie serves as a perfect example of this principle.

Sure—you might be able to hype yourself up mentally despite your consumption of junk food, but the probability of making long-term change life is nil because your body has been forced into a state of nutritional stress, which induces fear, anxiety, and a sense of lack.

Nature or Nurture? The Epigenetic Link between Diet and Mental State

In chapter 7, I introduced the concept of epigenetic research, which essentially states that we are in charge of our genetic expression and that we don't have to be bullied by our genetics. It's sobering to admit that we can no longer blame our genes for our disease or ailments and that we must take responsibility for our life. It's equally tempting to ignore the fact that nutrition is one of the biggest players in overall health. This includes mental, spiritual, emotional, social, intellectual, and physical health.

Just in case you're inclined to follow the Darwinian model of evolution, in which nature is presumed to be the dominant factor of genetic expression, consider that even Charles Darwin himself stated the following at the end of his life:

> In my opinion, the greatest error which I have committed has been not allowing sufficient weight to the direct action of the environment, i.e., food, climate, etc., independently of natural selection … When I wrote the *Origin*, and for some years afterwards, I could find little good evidence of the direct action of the environment; now there is a large body of evidence.

Obviously, Darwin became aware of how important the environment of the cell truly is. The physiological environment we provide our cells is largely determined by the quality of the food we choose to put in our mouth every time we open it. The other dominant players that determine our cellular environment are our thoughts and emotion. This points to the inextricable link between our physiology and psychology.

It's important to realize that both thoughts and food are forms of energy. The question you must ask yourself is "Am I consuming positive forms of both nutritional and thought energy?"

> The physiological environment we provide our cells
> is largely determined by the quality of the food we
> choose to put in our mouth every time we open it.

Now is the perfect time for you to face your nutritional habits squarely and realize that they have the power to influence your genetic expression profoundly. If you opt to eat natural wholesome foods, you aid your body in expressing the genes that affirm health. Alternatively, if you choose to take in processed food, you exponentially increase your chances of negatively altering your genetic makeup and expressing genes that negate health.

Artificial Foods Equals Artificial Thought: Simplify Your Nutrition Naturally

"Lose 30 pounds in 10 days!"

"Lose weight! No lifestyle modifications necessary!"

"The most revolutionary breakthrough in weight loss history!"

"Low-carb diet!"

"Low-fat diet!"

"Incinerate your fat while eating the foods you love!"

How many of these or similar diet slogans have you heard in your lifetime? How many times have you scratched your head in confusion as you observed how one diet contradicted the claims of another? How many infomercials have you seen with a doctor in a white coat and a stethoscope advocating a certain diet? How many times have you tried a diet, gotten discouraged because it was so restricting, and threw your hands up in the air and said, "Screw it! I'm going to eat whatever the hell I want!"

The simple fact is that nutrition does *not* have to be complex. We're the ones who make it complex by creating commercial diets, saying that certain natural foods are off limits (such as carbohydrates), and making as many new foods (processed foods) that the human mind can conceive. With these facts in mind, is it any wonder the average person gets confused about nutrition?

To better illustrate my point, let's go on a mental journey.

Let's go back in time to the fifteenth century. Do you think you would be able to enjoy the conveniences of modern nutrition? Where would you go for your favorite microwave popcorn? Where would you find the nearest convenient store to fuel your sugar addiction? Where would you drive-through to pick up your thirty-two ounces of sugar-laden soda? Where would you find Lunchables to feed your children? What fruit tree would provide you with juice boxes filled with your drink of choice?

Let's now imagine that it's breakfast time. As you sit down for breakfast, you're served eggs from the chickens that roam freely outside. Your eggs are accompanied by a glass of raw milk that came straight from the cow. You're also served some rice harvested from last year's crop. As you taste the food, you notice it is rich in texture and in flavor. Your taste buds are naturally drawn to the richness of the egg yolks and to the natural cream of the milk. You don't shudder at the sight of *real food*. And you don't think, *I wonder if I'm going to get sick from this unpasteurized milk?*

As you tackle your chores around the farm, you notice that your energy level is high and even-keeled. As noon approaches, your body becomes naturally hungry as your breakfast has been oxidized in the exertion of your chores. You decide to step inside for lunch. There you find herring, potatoes, and fresh butter. To top it off, you're served freshly cooked beets. You feel saliva coursing through your mouth in anticipation of eating. As you indulge in your meal, you once again revel in the natural flavor and satisfaction that the food brings. Your energy soars, and you're ready to outwork for the remainder of the afternoon.

Working outdoors, you notice a pear tree. Feeling tempted by the luscious shape and smell of its fruit, you pick one and devour it. Your taste buds are bathed in the naturally occurring sugars that Mother Nature has so lovingly allowed you to indulge in. Again you feel your appetite satisfied, and you notice that your sense of well-being is soaring.

As your workday comes to a close, you hear the cowbell ring as supper is served. You begin to salivate as you approach the house. As you get closer to the door, you're greeted by the enticing aroma of smoked pork. Sitting in your chair, you notice that the pork is topped with natural Parmesan cheese that was purchased at a local delicatessen.

To replenish your depleted energy, you're served buckwheat drizzled with olive oil and sauerkraut, and cucumber is served as a side dish. You look around and notice the people in the room getting a little giddy when dessert enters the room. You join the giddiness when you realize that homemade marzipan is about to be served.

You wash it all down with some fresh well water as you wind down for the evening. You feel clear headed and relaxed. You're excited to sit with your family, discuss life, and get ready for the next day. As you retire into a slumber for the night, you notice that you have no difficulty falling asleep and staying asleep. As you arise the next morning, you feel rejuvenated and ready to tackle the day.

Given this realistic scenario of the fifteenth century, I want to ask you some honest questions. If you indeed found yourself in a similar nutritional situation, would you be worried about the following?

- your weight
- when you should go on your next diet
- whether you are eating the "right" foods
- how many calories are in each of your meals
- whether the foods you're eating are approved by the latest nutritional expert or the FDA

I hope this story proves a simple yet significant point, and that point is this: Mother Nature designed you, and by so doing, she also designed your nutritional needs. In this naturally balanced nutritional state, there's no need for dieting, losing weight, or worrying about what foods are okay to consume.

We know without a doubt that naturally occurring nutritional states are divinely designed for our unique physiological needs. This knowledge is liberating, to say the least. It truly liberates us from the following:

- weight gain
- diseases of all kinds (diabetes, obesity, blood pressure disorders, etc.)
- dysfunctional thinking spurred by the negative physiological consequences of poor nutrition
- mood swings
- hormonal imbalances
- medical bills and health care costs
- excuse making

It's that simple. If we know that artificial and processed foods lead to the aforementioned list of ailments, it's safe to say that artificial foods contribute to artificial thinking, which is any form of thinking that's contrary to our natural state of being: peace, joy, contentment, and fulfillment.

A point of clarification: I'm the first to acknowledge that we're built to hold and express negative emotions, such as fear. These emotions are natural and useful, given the appropriate use of them, such as when the fight-or-flight system is activated.

Negative emotions become harmful only when they persist. They are perfectly appropriate when you're running for your life or experiencing legitimate relationship issues. They aren't appropriate in everyday life as a permanent way of thinking.

We have already covered how negative internal dialogues can be a learned way of living. When we allow a negative internal dialogue to persist, it has the power to take us out of our natural and God-given state of well-being. It would, no doubt, classify as artificial thinking.

We also can easily adopt artificial thinking through the consumption of artificial foods. As I stated earlier, those foods leads to stress within the body because the body perceives the food as foreign. It must take the food through a metabolic and detoxification process, which adds stress. As internal stress levels increase, so does negative thinking, which is the antithesis of our original nature. So we see how artificial food leads to artificial thinking.

> Eating artificial foods leads to stress within the body because the body perceives the food as foreign. It must take the food through a metabolic and detoxification process, which adds stress to the body. As internal stress levels increase, so does negative thinking, which is the antithesis of your original nature. So we see how artificial food leads to artificial thinking.

Undieting Your Diet:
Understanding Mother Earth versus Mother Science

The human diet was never intended to be complicated. With this truth in mind, I give you official permission never to worry about dieting again. Instead, eat wholesome and natural foods instead of processed and refined foods. You'll instinctively know when, where, and how much to eat. You won't have to worry about calorie counting, carb restriction, or commercial-driven mantras that happen to be popular

Let's agree on something right here and now. If I'm going to tell you to forget about dieting and further tell you that nutrition is simple, it's my responsibility to show you why this is true.

Imagine our ancestors at the dawn of humankind. What did they eat? Every nutritional need was taken care of through the bounty of Mother Earth. Fruits, vegetables, and animals were all available to nourish, fortify, and build human existence. Just as any mother nourishes her offspring, so does Mother Earth. It's no more complicated than this.

What foods Mother Earth provides:

- vegetables (both starchy and nonstarchy)
- fruits
- grains
- animals and animal products (such as dairy)

All these foods in their *whole*, unadulterated form should constitute 80 percent of your diet. The other 20 percent can come from what Mother Earth doesn't provide.

What foods Mother Earth doesn't provide:

- white flour or any white flour product (such as white bread, pasta, etc.)
- candy
- processed juices
- processed and refined canned goods
- processed (pasteurized/homogenized) dairy
- pastries
- energy drinks
- refined sugar
- processed fats (such as hydrogenated fats or processed vegetable oils)
- white refined salt
- any combination of white table sugar, salt, flour, or dairy (This includes *all* processed foods, which could include a list of more than thirty thousand that have been "invented" by the food-manufacturing industry.)

Always look at foods in two ways: those that come from the earth and those that were invented by a food scientist. When in doubt, simply trace the food's source by asking, "Did this food come from the earth or from a laboratory?" If you're still stumped, look at the label, and you'll quickly see either a short natural list of ingredients or a lengthy list of ingredients that will make your tongue do backflips when you try to pronounce them.

If after viewing the nonnatural list, you find yourself saying, "Well, Griff, many of those foods are made from *components* of naturally occurring foods," you're right. But you're missing the point. Foods should be consumed in their *whole* form, the way nature intended them. When you remove certain portions of a whole food and add foreign components, such as preservatives and artificial sweeteners, you denature the food, stripping it of the natural nutritional qualities your body is designed to consume.

The Food Processing Spectrum: Are You Living in Food Heaven or Food Hell?

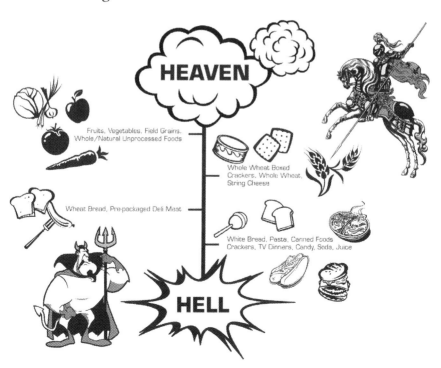

The term *processed food* is thrown around loosely these days, so it's important for you to know what to look for when selecting foods to eat. To make sense of this, look at my representation of food heaven and food hell above. Notice that whole foods reside in food heaven, and highly processed foods reside in food hell. Between the two extremes, you'll find foods that progressively become more processed as they approach food hell.

> A key principle that we often forget states that food
> is only as good as the nourishment it provides.

As simple as it would be to cast foods in two separate molds, one good and the other bad, all foods are meant to nourish the body. To the degree that they accomplish this, they become closer to food heaven. The food giants have sold us a big lie that has stripped us of our health. This lie purports that food is merely a fuel. You have no doubt heard statements such as "Fuel up before the big game!" Instead, we should be looking at the *nutrient profile* of food because food is only as good as the nourishment it provides.

To illustrate my point, let's look at one of the most commonly processed foods in the world: wheat. We could steer into complex issues here, such as gluten sensitivity, but my intention is to show you how this common grain traverses from food heaven to food hell through our food-processing procedures.

In its natural form, wheat has a rich nutrient profile, including vitamin E, manganese, selenium, enzymes, and fiber. This profile can vary according to the quality of the soil. My point here is that a whole grain carries with it the nutrition necessary to sustain life. A whole grain contains three parts: the bran, the germ, and the endosperm, all of which contribute to its overall nutrient profile.

When you see the term "whole wheat," know that the grain has been processed to a certain extent by milling, which breaks the whole grain down into a fine flour. This increases the surface area, which subsequently raises its glycemic index. This elevates blood sugar levels rapidly, which then leads to increased weight gain and insulin resistance if the pattern is repeated.

In addition, some of the kernel is removed, which takes away a portion of the germ and lowers fiber content. This is a perfect example of a food that is "minimally processed" yet carries with it nutritional and therefore physiological consequences.

Let's take this example a little further. In what's called "wheat bread," the whole grain has not only been milled and ground into fine flour, but it has been largely stripped of the bran and germ component. Manufacturers do intersperse some of these components back into the bread but only minimally.

Most wheat breads are made from enriched and refined flour that comes from stripping the whole wheat flour of its nutrients and then adding them back in via an artificial "enrichment" process. This version of bread resides in nutritional hell, though not in the depths.

In the depths is white bread. I don't refer to this product as a food, because every ounce of nutrition has been stripped out of it. To pass FDA regulations, this nutritionally bankrupt product is "enriched" or "fortified" with synthetic vitamins and minerals that the body often perceives as foreign and has a hard time absorbing. This leads to malnutrition, which leads to sugar cravings, ailments, and ultimately disease.

Eating foods in food hell commonly leads to the following problems:

- blood sugar issues (rapid elevations of blood sugar)
- muscle aches and pains (due to the lack of dietary enzymes and other nutrients in processed foods, which leads to food intolerance)
- hormonal imbalances (due primarily to imbalanced insulin-to-cortisol ratios)
- junk food cravings
- mood swings
- dehydration
- increased risk of cancer
- increased risk of heart disease
- blood lipid problems (HDL/LDL and triglyceride counts)

- Every negative physiological consequence that stems from imbalanced hormones—which accounts for hundreds of unexplained physical ailments.

The above list could fill pages of this book if I kept going. Many processed foods are on this spectrum of food heaven and hell, and it can get confusing at times to decipher what is good and what is bad.

Your Ultimate Solution

Again, my purpose is not to give you an exhaustive list of what foods are good and what foods are bad. That would require me an entire book. My job here is to teach you the fundamental principles that will bolster your health and remove your tendency to make excuses. The following very simple principles may strike you as simplistic, but if you follow them, you'll never need to worry about your nutrition again. Your diet will be building the physical body necessary to house your Highest Self.

Principle 1: Eat whole foods

Keep it simple; don't overthink. If it comes from the earth or from an animal in its natural form, it's probably okay to eat.

Principle 2: Ask the two questions

Before you eat, always ask these two questions:

1. Is the food natural? Where does it fall on the nutritional food heaven and food hell spectrum?
2. What is the glycemic index of this food?

If you answer the first question in the affirmative, you can almost rest assured that the glycemic index will be okay. This second question will help you be sure you're not pounding natural yet high-glycemic foods all day long. Examples include certain fruits, grains, or natural sugars. These in moderation are fine, but in excess, they can harm. To learn more about the glycemic index, read the book, *The New Glucose Revolution: The Authoritative Guide to the Glycemic Index.*

Principle 3: Don't be a fanatic. Live an eighty/twenty lifestyle

I've met countless people who love to get on a diet kick and go all out. Most of these people are driven, motivated, inspired, and righteous about their pursuits—until they aren't. Inevitably they burn out and resort back to previous dietary practices and excuses.

You must be honest with yourself and make sure you're truly eating healthy, whole foods 80 percent of the time so you can reserve the other 20 percent for an occasional treat and/or processed food. The eighty/twenty rule may work differently for different people. For some, it means eating clean every weekday and then having a cheat meal on the weekend. For others, it means eating healthy throughout the day but allowing a treat such as ice cream or a candy bar. Either way is appropriate to the eighty/twenty rule. Just make sure you're honest with yourself. This is an easy rule to bend, contort, distort, or break all together.

Principle 4: Eat Right for Your Metabolic Type

Have you ever noticed that certain people have dietary needs and/or desires that seem weird? For example, you may naturally be drawn to carbohydrate sources, such as whole grains, starches, and fruits, while your best friend may be drawn to protein and fat-rich foods, such as meat, nuts, cheeses, and oils. You may have labeled these people as unhealthy because they don't conform to a conventional low-fat diet.

Our bodies are designed for different ratios of fuel (carbs, protein, and fat), depending on our genetic disposition. I've studied and implemented this in my life and in the lives of my clients with wonderful results. The foremost expert on this topic is William Wolcott, who has written a fantastic book, *The Metabolic Typing Diet,* on understanding your own unique metabolism.

Principle 5: Hydrate Up!

An explanation of the importance of hydration could fill hundreds of pages. One of the best books on this topic is *Your Body's Many Cries for Water* by Dr. F. Batmanghelidj. It's a must-read if you want to understand proper hydration in relation to your health.

Well, there you have it, my friend—all the simple principles you'll ever need to make sure that you're creating a *physiological* environment that leads you into a place of *psychological* bliss. In this state of bliss, personal power will prevail, and excuses will fade.

Remember that your body is your temple; it houses the consciousness of your Highest Self. It is now your responsibility to respect and feed your temple with the foods that will allow you to resonate and live in a state of health and well-being.

CHAPTER 14

EXCUSE EXORCISM 5

Unwinding Your Mind and Feeling Sublime

Exorcizing Your Excuses by Doing More of Nothing

Where there is peace and meditation, there is neither anxiety nor doubt.
—St. Francis de Sales

I want to make a full disclosure: I struggle with rest and with unwinding my ever-hyper mind. I anticipate that I have yet to see and experience the full value of this principle as I seek to balance my own work-to-rest ratio.

Imagine that you're a kid again, and step into your brain. What do you see? Do you see a calm lake undisturbed by wind, rain, or snow? What do you hear? Do you hear silence and peace? Do you peer inside your brain and see both hemispheres (left and right) cooperating with one another, creating movement and harmony? Does your brain resemble a forest with seemingly random thoughts creating the perfection that only nature can create?

Chances are good that the above scenario is not a reality for you right now. Looking in from the top of your brain, you don't see the clear lake; rather, you see a whirlwind of unrelated information swirling around endlessly. As you zoom in on this information, you realize that you continually utter thoughts, scripts, and dialogues to yourself day in and day out.

You catch one of your favorite dialogues, which reads, "I am incapable of change. I've tried to change, and I've always failed." You smile in agreement and continue to read your internal dialogues.

As you move near to your ears, you can hear your inner dialogues. You become confused as you listen to the conflicting chatter that you've formed over the years. You observe that some of your chatter is positive and life affirming, but you quickly observe that 90 percent of it is negative and self-defeating.

As you continue to traverse the terrain of your brain, you hear tones of frustration, anticipation, and hopelessness. Reality begins to settle in, and you conclude that your brain is confused by loud and conflicting messages. You hear tones of stress, and you see thoughts everywhere that are laced with stress and anxiety.

As you observe both the left and right hemispheres of your brain, you notice something peculiar: the left side has smoke coming out of it due to overuse. And you notice that your right side is sleeping soundly in the corner, sucking its thumb.

Although these metaphorical stories may seem farfetched, would you agree that the latter description is more indicative of most people living in our modern world? We're in a constant hurry to meet deadlines and expectations, to maintain relationships, and to do our jobs. If allowed to persist, this state quickly turns our lives into a reality that's stressful and unpleasant. If we look at this from a spiritual perspective, it begs the question "Can I live as my Highest Self under these conditions?"

The fact is that we live busy lives, and we stress ourselves out far too much. We are afflicted by a cultural disease that continues to dominate our lives. Subconsciously, most people today wear their stress card as a badge of honor. To prove this, think of the last time somebody asked you how you were doing, and you instinctively said, "I'm good—just really busy." We tend to measure our productivity, professionalism, and self-worth by how busy and/or how stressed we are.

The by-product of an overly busy life is an overly busy mind, and an overly busy mind invites and creates stress. Excessive stress creates a physiological environment that's conducive to excuse making. When we become overly stressed, we place our body into fight-or-flight mode. *And our brain naturally sifts and filters out any extraneous information that is not deemed crucial for survival.*

This is great for survival, but it sucks for setting and achieving goals because goals are deemed to be unnecessary for survival. Your brain says, "I'm concerned with surviving, not thriving!"

> The by-product of an overly busy life is an overly busy mind, and an overly busy mind invites and creates stress. Excessive stress creates a physiological environment that's conducive to excuse making.

People in survival mode have closed down their creative juices and put personal development on hold so they can deal with stress. But a dirty little secret you absolutely must know is that the mind can never deal with all its perceived stressors until it slows down and processes them. When your mind is running a million miles per hour, it can't focus on anything, and when it can't focus, it can't process relevant, empowering information that is necessary for personal change.

The Dynamic Duo of Your Nervous System: Where Stress Is Stored

"I am stressed out!" Have you ever considered what this statement means? Are you truly aware of how stress affects your physical body and health? You may have heard people say that they store stress in their shoulders or neck. Is this possible? Is stress tangible or intangible? Can the body actually store stress?

We must answer these questions and find methods of dissipating excessive stress so we can live in resonance with our Highest Self. We must reconcile ourselves with the fact that we can't resonate with or operate from our Highest Self when excessive stress dominates our life.

We must reconcile ourselves with the fact that we can't resonate with or operate from our Highest Self when excessive stress dominates our life.

Stress comes from various sources. In his book, *How to Eat, Move and Be Healthy!* Paul Chek breaks stress into six primary categories:

1. Physical
2. Chemical
3. Electomagnetic
4. Psychic (mental/emotional)
5. Nutritional
6. Thermal

Physical stress is incurred at the physical level, and it stems from both external and internal sources. Consider weightlifting as an example of *external* physical stress. When you lift heavy weights, the weight bears down on your body and creates a positive form of physical stress.

It may seem paradoxical, but *internal* stress often results from a lack of exercise. The lack of appropriate external stress often leads to various forms of internal stress. These internal stresses often manifest as osteoporosis, lowered red blood cell counts, hormonal imbalances, muscle weakening, and postural decline.

Chemical stress can also be caused by external and internal sources. External sources include environmental pollution such as pesticides, herbicides, and fungicides. All these sources can enter your body through the air, water, and food. Internal forms of chemical stress include the overproduction of stress hormones, such as cortisol or adrenaline. These stress hormones often manifest through negative thinking patterns, adding to your internal stress burden.

When we allow ourselves to revel in negative thinking, we give our body no choice but to produce an overabundance of stress hormones that are toxic to our body. The liver is then forced to detoxify these hormones, which adds further stress to our body's systems.

Electromagnetic stress emanates from sunlight, radio waves, sound waves, and a wide variety of electromagnetic waves used in everything from cell phones to MRI scanners. In excess, these waves can disrupt a body's delicate electromagnetic balance.

Psychic stress is more popularly known as mental or emotional stress. This is what most people lump all the forms of stress under because we don't realize that there are actually five forms of stress. I'm almost certain that you are very well acquainted with psychic of stress and could spend hours telling me about it. It ranges from the stress that we feel from an approaching deadline to the stress of a relationship that's heading south.

Broadly speaking, we incur psychic stress when our expectations aren't met. To use a silly example, let's say you believe you should be happy and never experience disappointment. This faulty belief practically guarantees psychic stress when you experience circumstances that are contrary to your expectation.

Every time we take something into our body, we create nutritional stress. The stress can be good or bad, depending on the food we select. For example, eating highly processed foods creates a high amount of physiological stress for your body. That's because your body is forced to detoxify the added flavorings and chemicals that it wasn't intended to ingest.

Alternatively, when you eat a whole food from a natural source, it provides your body with a stress that's necessary for optimal living. Much of this stress comes from the metabolism of the nutrients in the food. It takes energy to convert carbohydrate into glucose, break down fibers, and utilize vitamins and minerals.

We incur thermal stress when our body temperature gets too high or too low. This can stem from a lack of exercise, too much exercise, sunburn, a lack of heavy clothing in a cold climate, and so forth.

Remember that none of these forms of stress is inherently good or bad. It is the excess or absence that creates excessive stress in the body. Consider that most people equate exercise with good stress that supports the body. Although this assumption is correct, too much exercise with too little rest can be very damaging.

All these stressors need to be *balanced* if you hope to exorcise your excuses. If you carry excessive stress in *any* of these areas, it will be very difficult to make long-term changes. Take a moment to review the descriptions of each type of stress, and make a mental note of what areas are troubling you.

So, there you have it. You now know that your body takes in six basic forms of stress. You may now be asking, *Where does my body store all this stress, and does it differentiate the six different forms? Are there six different containers for all six forms?*

The human body is not capable of differentiating forms of stress. It's concerned only with stress as a whole. It makes no difference where the stress is coming from, be it mental, emotional, or electromagnetic. Many people make the error of thinking that since they have low mental or emotional stress, they are stress-free. These same people could have a high degree of nutritional, physical, and chemical stress that adds to their overall stress burden.

> The human body is not capable of differentiating forms of stress. It's concerned only with stress as a whole. It makes no difference where the stress is coming from, be it mental, emotional, or electromagnetic.

Your total stress burden is housed and stored in your nervous system. This fact often sneaks up and bites people on the butt. Your nervous system is affected by all six forms of stress, and if they're left unmanaged, disease will result. As mentioned in the previous chapter, there are two branches of the autonomic nervous system: the sympathetic branch and the parasympathetic branch.

Yin and Yang: Are You "Yanged Out?"

You may have seen the yin and yang symbol above. The Chinese have incorporated the concept of yin and yang in their collective lifestyle and in their practice of medicine for thousands of years. The underlying principle behind yin and yang is balance; every facet of life needs balance to sustain homeostasis. For example, if you're always on the run, and your sleep suffers as a result, your body will eventually force you to slow down by getting sick or diseased. Nature always balances the forces of yin and yang, whether they're pleasant or unpleasant. And *you* are a part of nature.

So how do stress and stress management relate to yin and yang? As I just mentioned, your autonomic (or automatic) nervous system has two primary branches. The sympathetic branch is in charge of regulating hormones and neurotransmitters that prime your body for fight or flight. It also helps you to stay active and alert so you can live life and accomplish the tasks of daily living. So this branch of your nervous system is an integral part of your human experience and is necessary for your very survival. This is the yang portion of your nervous system.

> Nature always balances the forces of yin and yang, whether they're pleasant or unpleasant. And you are a part of nature.

In short, your sympathetic nervous system is your internal green light that allows you to go, go, go.

In contrast, your parasympathetic nervous system initiates a sense of calm within you and encourages you to relax and recover from your daily grind. It serves as your red light. It helps regulate key hormones and neurotransmitters that allow your body to relax, rejuvenate, and receive the rest it needs to function optimally. This is the yin portion of your nervous system.

It's imperative to understand that these two branches of your nervous system serve opposite but equal functions, and they need to remain balanced for optimal health. It's possible for one branch of the nervous system to dominate the other. I'll give you one guess which one is dominant in our Western culture. You guessed it, the sympathetic. It's the undisputed champion of our physiology. We have essentially "yanged" ourselves out with busy schedules, self-imposed demands, and deadlines. In so doing, we've disrupted the delicate balance of yin and yang energy and are suffering the consequences.

To be yanged out is to be sympathetic dominant. Below is a very limited list of ailments and diseases that can results from this yin-yang (or nervous system) imbalance:

- anxiety/anxiousness
- digestion issues
- fungal infections in the gut
- immune system compromise (you get sick often and for extended periods)
- nagging coughs
- adrenal fatigue
- general fatigue and irritability
- malnourishment due to nutrient malabsorption
- sleeping disturbances/insomnia
- low libido / sex drive
- increased risk of cancer, stroke, and heart attack

The quagmire we find ourselves in stems from our addiction to sympathetic dominance. This addiction comes from societal expectations, pressures, and norms. We've defined success as the accumulation of material wealth, and we've burned ourselves out pursuing it. I'm all for success when it's defined and balanced by the needs and desires of our Higher Self. But sympathetic dominance often results when we ignore the inner promptings of our Higher Self and therefore subjugate ourselves to the materialistic desires and whims of our ego.

In the previous chapter, I briefly described how poor nutritional choices could favor a dominance of sympathetic activity. In addition, our thoughts, sleep patterns, exercise habits, and lack of spiritual focus can lead to a state of sympathetic overload. When these areas are left unbalanced, it can lead to accumulated stress stored in your nervous system. When your nervous system gets overloaded by any of the six forms of stress mentioned earlier, it manifests through dis-ease in your body.

> I'm all for success when it's defined and balanced by the
> needs and desires of our Higher Self. Sympathetic dominance
> often results when we ignore the inner promptings of
> our Higher Self and therefore subjugate ourselves to
> the materialistic desires and whims of our ego.

You might be asking, "What can I do about all this stress in my life?" That's a very good question. The answer is multifaceted, and each chapter of this book represents part of the overall solution. Now let's look at a fundamental truth concerning the solution by introducing a paradox few people understand.

Do Nothing to Get Everything Done!
The Benefits of Slowing the Mind

If I were to gather five hundred people in a room and ask how many of them led a busy life, at least 90 percent would raise their hands. I can state this with confidence because I've done it with every audience I've spoken to—albeit in smaller numbers.

In our society, we believe in linear logic and black-and-white thinking. This always emanates from left-brain dominance. To illustrate this, imagine what you would think if I were to give you a long list of chores and then tell you to do none of them. That's what I'm going to ask you to do here.

On the surface, it may seem absurd to suggest that you can get everything done by doing nothing. We all know that action must be taken for anything to get done. Yet it is still true that *more* will get done by doing nothing.

Most people approach their daily tasks with a brain jumbled and garbled with too much information. They simply have too many conditioned beliefs combined with external stimuli swirling around in their head— to the point that they can't focus. This is a mental symptom of being sympathetically overdrawn and stressed out.

Here is a surefire way to find out if you need to slow your mind. Stop what you're doing right now—this second. Shut off your cell phone, get rid of all distraction, and seclude yourself in nature or at least in a silent room. Close your eyes and get into a comfortable position so you can breathe freely through your nose. Now for the hard part. Focus *solely* on your breathing. Allow no thoughts. The only thing you're allowed to think about is your breathing—and your breathing only!

Now it's time for some honest answers. How long did you last before you started having thoughts that had nothing to do with your breathing? Regardless of where your thoughts took you, I'm almost certain that you struggled to focus on your breath alone. Did it feel as though there were two sharks stuck in your brain that were determined to get out? If you experienced anything similar to this, you are left-brain dominant and therefore sympathetically dominant in your nervous system. This is creating undue stress and robbing you of the stillness of mind that you deserve.

While you're under these conditions, it's impossible to process information on a global level and see "the whole picture." To illustrate my point, think of your brain as a high-powered video camera. If I were to rip this page out of the book and put it in front of you, place you two feet away from it, stick a video camera in your hand, and ask you to read me the entire page, would you be able to?

Your ability to do it would be contingent on one key feature on the camcorder: the zoom button. If you zoomed out, you'd be able to read the entire page. But if you zoomed in, you'd see only a few words—and would be unable to make sense of what the page was trying to convey. You wouldn't be able to understand what my book was teaching, because you would be unable to focus on the big picture.

In like fashion, when our mind is spinning a million miles per second, it's nearly impossible to focus on the big picture of life—or our Crystal-Clear Vision, as discussed earlier. When we can't focus on our CCV, it's easy to get overwhelmed and flustered. This happens because our conscious mind tries to focus on multiple items at once, which is an impossible task, because the conscious mind can focus on only one thing. The antithesis of our conscious mind is our subconscious mind, which can process thousands of bits of information per second. In fact, the ability of the subconscious mind to process information is almost limitless.

Here is the problem: We typically draw from our traffic-jammed conscious mind to accomplish all our goals. We then get frustrated because nothing gets done due to our lack the ability to focus. In contrast, when we draw from the power of our right brain, which houses our subconscious and superconscious mind, we can harness its nearly limitless power and become infinitely more productive. In essence, we are "zooming out" so we can see the whole picture and make informed decisions based on that picture.

When you're able to see the big picture of life, your CCV is naturally captured by your subconscious mind. When you combine your CCV with repetition and emotion, as described in chapters 8 and 9, you begin to reprogram your subconscious mind so it aids you in your desires, dreams, and goals.

This is where slowing your mind comes to your rescue. Through meditation, your superconscious mind or Higher Self is accessed, and your subconscious mind is reprogrammed. In this moment of silence, you commune with your Highest Self and receive divine guidance.

> Through meditation, your superconscious mind or Higher Self is accessed, and your subconscious mind is reprogrammed. In this moment of silence, you commune with your Highest Self and receive divine guidance.

When you routinely slow your mind through meditation and commune with your Highest Self, you experience the following benefits:

- lowered blood pressure
- lowered blood glucose
- lowered cholesterol
- increased sense of being centered or grounded
- increased ability to focus on and process information
- mood enhancement
- increased stress management
- end of breathing disorders (breathing disorders can cause a host of physical problems)
- increased ability to concentrate
- increased ability to be present with others in intimate and social settings
- relaxed muscles
- balance of the sympathetic and parasympathetic branches of the nervous system
- enhanced positive emotions and perceptions
- connection to your soul or your Highest Self
- satiated spiritual needs and desires
- slower life that you can enjoy
- connection to your superconscious mind, or all-knowing Source, for problem solving (If you think this sounds hokey, how do you explain Einstein, Edison, and other geniuses who came up with new equations and inventions?)
- balanced hormones
- slower breathing rate and deep diaphragmatic breathing

- removal from the grind of everyday living
- enhanced ability to access your subconscious
- enhanced sleeping rhythms, patterns, and depth
- an ability to be happy and more pleasant to be around
- fun, relaxation, and adventure

Did you know that sleep is one of your most powerful tools in accomplishing most of the above? As a nation, we lack sleep, and we're reaping the physiological and psychological consequences. The human body requires at least eight hours of sleep per night. It's also wise to get to bed at the same time each night so your body can establish a sleeping pattern and rhythm. An optimal sleeping pattern is getting to bed by ten thirty and getting up by six thirty. This ensures that your body has the chance to recover from your daily routine both physically and mentally.

Without adequate sleep, you can meditate until the cows come home but experience little to no results. It's impossible to overstate how important sleep is for slowing your mind and balancing your physiology. It allows you to start your day with a clean slate so you can truly exorcise your excuses.

Three meditative techniques can help you slow your mind and balance your body. This chapter isn't meant to give you a formal guide to meditation or sleep but to educate you about their important in the pursuit of exorcising your excuses. There are many excellent resources available on meditation, and I encourage you to find a resource that resonates with you and helps you to sustain this vital practice.

Reyinifying Your Life: Simple Meditation Techniques

Meditative Practice 1: Breathing Meditation

This form of meditation is perfect if you're new to meditation. Sit or lie in a comfortable position so you can breathe freely. If you're sitting, be sure to maintain a posture that allows for deep diaphragmatic inhalation. This will require that you sit upright in a semierect posture, but do not force it.

Remember you're trying to get your body to relax at all levels. My favorite position for this exercise is lying on my back.

Once you're in a comfortable position, begin to breathe in through your nose. As you do so, be sure you're breathing with your diaphragm, which should serve as your natural breathing muscle. If, when you breathe, you find that your chest expands before your belly, you're using muscles that aren't designed for breathing. If you find breathing through your diaphragm difficult, you might have a breathing disorder.

To correct this disorder, simply breathe through your nose and imagine the air racing into your belly. Imagine that you're channeling the air into your belly as you watch your belly expand. Your chest should rise only after you have inhaled to about 75 percent of your max inhalation capacity. Count ten to sixteen breaths per minute, depending on your level of cardiovascular fitness.

For an example of functional breathing, watch children breathe. They aren't wound up with stress, nor do they suffer from a hyperactive mind, which causes dysfunctional breathing in the adult population. It will take some time and practice to correct your dysfunctional breathing, but it will be well worth it for your health and well-being.

When comfortable and breathing correctly, focus on the air coming in through your nose and exiting through your nose or mouth. *The goal is to quiet your mind by* not *thinking about anything except your breath*. It may help to direct your focus to the base of your nose when inhaling. I like to sense the air moving in and out of my nose and lungs. I remain aware of inner sensations associated with the air coursing through my body.

When you start this practice, you'll probably find your mind wandering off. I've practiced this version of meditation on and off for nearly twelve years, and I still have to catch my mind when it wanders. The key is not to let your ego into the picture by judging yourself. Simply acknowledge that you're veering off, and bring your attention back to your breathing. Focus on the deep, relaxing, and fulfilling breaths that you're experiencing.

Many mystics and spiritual teachers have stated that proper breathing is the gateway between the conscious and the superconscious mind. Mediation serves as the bridge between your body and your soul.

Remember that your ability to focus on your breathing to the exclusion of thoughts determines how much your left brain relaxes and how much your right brain connects to your superconscious mind.

> *Mediation serves as the bridge between your body and your soul.*

When you first try this practice, three minutes is likely to feel impossible. If you're wound up and left-brain dominant, it may feel like torture, and you may find your mind saying, *This is a huge waste of time, and it's silly.* If you have these thoughts, be patient with yourself and work up to greater lengths. Ironically, the more you have these thoughts, the more you need to slow your brain down. Remember not to overwhelm yourself, and remember that initially three minutes is great. Eventually increase to twenty minutes and beyond when possible.

To recap, follow these simple steps:

1. Find a quiet place where you will not be disturbed.
2. Sit or lie in a comfortable position.
3. Begin to inhale through your nose into your belly. Your chest should rise only after you have inhaled 75 percent of your max air.
4. Focus on the air moving into and out of your nose. Imagine it coursing down into your belly so that it expands.
5. If your mind wanders, forgive yourself without judgment, and pull your attention back to your breathing.
6. Work up to twenty minutes or more if desired. If you're a beginner, three to five minutes is a good starting place. But be sure to steadily increase your duration to a *minimum* of twenty minutes.

Meditative Practice 2*: Superconscious Sleeping Meditation*

The purpose of this meditation is to gain maximum access to your superconscious mind while prepping your body for a deep and relaxing sleep. To perform this meditation, incorporate a wind-down routine into your nightly routine. I recommend turning off all electronics and bright lights at least one hour before bedtime, and implement a form of relaxation such as music, nontoxic candles, or a bath with Epsom salt or lavender. The key is to get your sympathetic nervous system to relax and allow your parasympathetic nervous system to dominate.

When you're relaxed and feeling a little drowsy, turn off your lights and close your eyes. Begin to take deep diaphragmatic breaths as outlined above in the first meditative practice. When you begin to breathe rhythmically, feel yourself drifting off. When this happens, bring your focus onto a question or a problem you need to solve. Hold this question or problem in your mind, and continue to breathe diaphragmatically.

The goal is to take on the role of a bystander. As a bystander, you immerse yourself into a state of being rather than thinking. You're sending your question into the cosmos or universe and fully expecting an answer in return. Remember you are the *observer*, not the thinker.

Take note of any inspired thoughts, insights, and intuitions that come into your mind as a result of being the observer. This is an excellent method of meditation if you're seeking answers in your life. Don't be shy! Remember your soul is your Highest Self, and as such, it's willing and able to guide you. After all, your soul is all-knowing and has your best interest at heart because it comes from a place of unconditional love.

You can also perform this meditation during the daytime. Consider doing either at eleven in the morning or three in the afternoon, when most people's bodies experience a natural dip in energy. This allows you to meditate when your body is naturally amenable to rest. This method of meditation is also best done in a dark quiet room or in nature.

Try holding a metal spoon in your hand while you drape your arm over the bed or chair. Put a metal pan (like a cookie sheet) under it, so you can hear the spoon fall if you drop off. This will wake you up if you accidentally fall asleep.

> Remember—your soul is your Highest Self, and as such, it's willing and able to guide you. After all, your soul is all-knowing and has your best interest at heart because it comes from a place of unconditional love.

You'll be amazed at the depth and quality of sleep that ensues after this form of meditation and at the insights that come into your consciousness from your Highest Self. Take note of them, and honor them by implementing them immediately. Wise men and women always listen when God speaks to their soul.

To recap, follow these simple steps:

1. Implement a wind-down routine at night in preparation for bed.
2. Shut off the lights, and allow yourself to lie close to the edge of the bed.
3. Hold a spoon in your hand with a metal pan (like a cookie sheet) underneath it so it alerts you if you fall asleep.
4. Begin to breathe deeply as outlined in the first meditative practice.
5. When you feel yourself drifting, quickly pose a question to your soul, such as "What should I do for a career?" Keep in mind that you can ask *any* question.
6. Be the observer. The goal here is to *not* think. Your superconscious mind will place thoughts, insights, intuitions, and intentions into your conscious mind. Observe and record these personal insights and inspirations.

Meditative Practice 3: Contract-Relax Meditation

This is a great method if you have achy muscles and/or a wound-up mind. To perform this meditation, sit in a chair with an upright yet relaxed posture or lie on the floor.

Inhale through your nose and take a deep diaphragmatic breath. At the peak of your inhalation, tense the muscles of your feet. Get them to the point of near exhaustion, and then let them relax entirely as you exhale.

Focus on the sensation of your muscles as you take them through the contraction and relaxation phase. Feel the tightness as you contract and also feel the blood rush in as you relax.

Repeat this pattern with all your muscles. When you're done with your feet, progress up to your calf muscles. When you're done with your calves, it's time to progress to your quadriceps and hamstrings. Progressively move up your body until you reach the muscles of your face. When you finish, relax and rest for a moment. Then, in a single momentous effort, contract your entire body.

After contracting your entire body, relax. Be sure to relax both your mind and your body. This is extremely important to remember because you're incurring both a physiological and psychological benefit from this technique. Allow your muscles and your mind to focus on *nothing*! Literally melt into the floor, and savor how good it feels to relax and do nothing. Focus only on your breathing and your nothingness.

To recap, follow these simple steps:

1. Sit in a chair or lie on the floor on your back.
2. Take deep diaphragmatic breaths until you feel relaxed and calm.
3. At the peak of your next inhalation, contract the muscles of your feet and hold for three to five seconds.
4. When you exhale, release all tension in your feet, and allow your mind to relax as well. Focus only on your breathing, as outlined in the first method of meditation.
5. Repeat the process with your calf muscles, and then work upward until you reach the muscles of your face.
6. Tense all the muscles of the body, and then allow your muscles and mind to relax as you exhale into a state of nothingness.

If properly performed, this should take anywhere from fifteen to twenty minutes

There are literally dozens of meditative techniques. In addition to meditation, yoga, tai chi, qigong, and other spiritual practices and light martial arts are engineered perfectly to help slow your mind. If these methods seem to daunting to you, do something as simple as a meditative walk in nature. When taking a meditative walk, breathe deeply and to focus your mind. Meditation doesn't have to be complicated, nor should it be. And I'm convinced that there's a meditative technique for everybody. Your job is to find the method that resonates with your soul.

Now it's time to implement what you've learned by quieting your mind. Meditation is a practice that few people take advantage of, yet it's a key element in rebalancing your life both mentally and physiologically. This is your chance to elevate your life to a higher spiritual plane—a place in which you find your Higher Self. Enjoy.

CHAPTER 15

EXCUSE EXORCISM 6

Exercising Your Body to Exorcize Your Excuses

The Mesmerizing Magic of Movement

*In order for man to succeed in life, God provided him with two means,
education and physical activity. Not separately, one for the soul and
the other for the body, but for the two together. With these two means,
man can attain perfection.*
—Plato

Life is energy. Life is change. Life is movement! The last six centuries of history validate these statements. Specifically, in the 1600s, Sir Isaac Newton established certain laws of physics, now called Newtonian physics. Centuries later, Albert Einstein developed the theory of relatively, which opened the doors to a modern way of thinking—namely, quantum physics.

I have studied the basics of quantum physics enough to know that everything in our universe can be boiled down to one substance: *energy*. Energy animates our entire universe. It makes no difference if we're talking about the composition of a human being or of an atomic bomb, because everything on this planet, be it living or nonliving, comes from the same stuff—energy. In simplistic terms, the only thing that differentiates a human being from an atom bomb is its pattern of energy and how fast it vibrates.

If you're scratching your head and asking why this is important, I'll answer your question by asking you a few questions. What do you think your body is made of? What do you think your brain is made of? What do you think your thoughts, emotions, and feelings are made of? Yup, you guessed it. Energy! Whether we're talking about a tangible body or an intangible thought, they're all made of energy. The tangible "you" and your intangible thoughts interact and influence one another every second of every day.

We are intelligently organized bundles of energy divided into energy systems. Each system is named in anatomical terms, such as brain, heart, and lungs. The proper and efficient interaction of these energetic systems allows you to function optimally and to maintain ideal health and wellness. As an energetic being, your body is a conduit and conductor of energy. Energy from your food, your thoughts, and your environment flows into your body from your head to your toes. It then traverses each and every one of your cells.

When this flow of energy is blocked or hampered in any way, disease—or dis-ease—results. Dis-ease is the result of either too much energy moving through your system or not enough. For thousands of years, acupuncturists and other energy healers have worked successfully to apply this principle.

What does this energy talk have to do with exorcizing your excuses? We've confirmed that our excuses come from our brains. *Our brains are continually producing thoughts that are heavily influenced by our biochemistry.* This is an extremely important statement because our biochemistry is continually influenced by food, exercise, water, sleep schedules, and thoughts.

In short, *everything* in life is movement. From your muscle fibers producing movement, to your neurons transmitting information from cell to cell, to your heart beating blood, to your endocrine system producing hormones— your body is constantly moving. You are hardwired to move physically, emotionally, mentally, and spiritualty, and when you experience optimal movement in these areas, you experience health, well-being, and fulfillment. When movement in these areas becomes stagnant, dis-ease results, and disease follows.

> Our biochemistry is continually influenced by food,
> exercise, water, sleep schedules, and thoughts.

Every chapter in this book is devoted to describing how physical, emotional, mental, and spiritual *nonmovement* leads to excuse making. For example, if your nutrition is stagnant, you will incur a host of physical ailments that make it very difficult to be optimistic and joyful. The same can be said for negative internal dialogues, lack of vision, lack of goals, or not getting enough time for yourself. *Each of these states of being creates nonmovement, which leads to a life riddled with excuses and alibis.*

> You are hardwired to move physically, emotionally, mentally,
> and spiritualty, and when you experience optimal movement in
> these areas, you experience health, well-being, and fulfillment.

Now that you're aware of the benefits of emotional, mental, and nutritional movement and how they create an environment conducive to personal power, let's look at the physical benefits associated with the movement and exercise of your greatest earthly gift: *your body.*

Building Your Mental Infrastructure: Physically Fortifying Your Brain against Excuse Making

Let's take a look at what houses our thoughts. To do this, we must first understand the basic nature of thought transmission—the ability of the brain to pass a thought through its electrical circuitry.

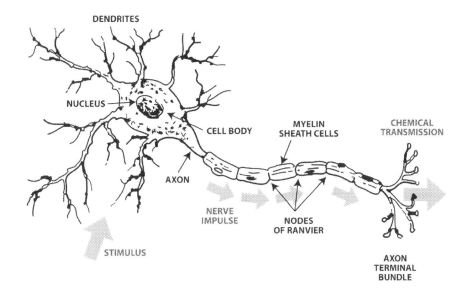

As the illustration above suggests, a brain neuron is responsible for passing energy in the form of a thought from neuron to neuron. These highly specialized brain cells have branch-like tentacles at their extremities, which are called dendrites. They also have a cell body and nucleus. From the nucleus extends a long, whiplike conduction channel called the axon. At the end of the axon lies a bundle of nerve fibers called the axon terminal bundle, which connects into the next neuron cell via a synaptic gap (not shown in the illustration).

Some experts have suggested that this process of nerve transmission (or thought transmission) is equivalent to the speed of light. Regardless of the actual speed, trying to pass a *new* empowering thought through a worn-down brain cell is analogous to crossing a bridge that was built in the 1700s during wartime. You aren't going to get far!

The stark reality that we all must understand is this: If our brain cells are weak, we have a weak physical infrastructure that isn't conducive to learning or new behaviors. This is a tremendous barrier to exorcising your excuses because learning new habits is the essence of personal development.

Science has shown that your brain must be physically strong before it can be mentally strong. To put it in automotive terms, you can't have Ferrari thoughts with a Pinto infrastructure. Remember you're learning how to think differently. All the excuse exorcisms that you're reading about in this book are designed to help you reprogram your brain both metaphysically (energetically) and physically.

You might be asking, "How do I strengthen my brain's physical infrastructure so I can reprogram it?" The answer is multifaceted. Researchers have found that continuing education and self-efficacy can help bolster the physical structure of the brain. Self-efficacy is your level of self-confidence specific to a task or life skill. This has been common knowledge for many years. What has not been common knowledge until recently is that exercise literally helps to rebuild your brain cells' infrastructure.

To understand this, we must realize that our brain is the home of countless neurotransmitters that aid in the thinking process. They're responsible for signaling from cell to cell, as described above, but they aren't responsible for the physical infrastructure of the cell. This is the job of a class of factors, the most important of which is called the brain-derived neurotrophic factor (BDNF). This substance is largely responsible for the physical growth and maintenance of brain cell structure.

In his best-selling book *Spark,* John J. Ratey, MD, describes what happens to neurons when sprinkled with BDNF:

> Early on, researchers found that if they sprinkled BDNF onto neurons in a petri dish, the cells automatically sprouted new branches, producing the same structural growth required for learning—and causing me to think of BDNF as Miracle Gro for the brain.[12]

If you aren't excited about this knowledge, you should be. We just learned that BDNF is largely responsible for building the physical infrastructure of your brains neurons. This is *extremely* important because without a healthy

---

[12] John J. Ratey, MD, *Spark: The Revolutionary New Science of Exercise and the Brain* (New York: Little, Brown and Company, 2008).

and strong brain, you'll never get rid of your excuses. You'll simply lack the strength and vitality to do so.

Again, exercise is largely responsible for building or rebuilding your brain's infrastructure. Researcher Carl Cotman showed that rats that received exercise, when compared to their sedentary counterparts, had higher levels of BDNF in their hippocampus—an area of the brain that is highly involved in the learning process—than their sedentary counterparts.

To summarize, if our brains don't possess the ability to make new neurons, we don't have the ability to take in new information and learn a new way of thinking. If we don't have the ability to take in new information, we surrender ourselves to the bondage of old thinking habits. The infrastructure of our brain neurons must change before we can change. It is that simple. So exercise that encourages BDNF production allows for the proper building and maintenance of a healthy brain.

> If our brains don't possess the ability to make new neurons, we don't have the ability to take in new information and learn a new way of thinking. If we don't have the ability to take in new information, we surrender ourselves to the bondage of old thinking habits. The infrastructure of our brain neurons must change before we can change. It is that simple.

It's illogical to think that exercise alone will produce a healthy brain capable of champion-level thinking. Nutrition, sleep, time to yourself, and internal dialogues all contribute to the physical structure of your brain

> Exercise that encourages BDNF production allows for the proper building and maintenance of a healthy brain.

Correcting Your Corrosive Cortisol

Why do you make excuses? Why do you feel the need to excuse away the things that you know you should be doing? What is the driving force behind each and every one of your excuses?

As human beings, we are designed to seek pleasure and to avoid pain. The simple fact is that we are meant to experience stress, but we aren't meant to experience excessive and chronic stress. When we experience chronic stress, we fall into a state of dis-ease that leads us to psychological and physiological dysfunction. A dysfunctional mind leads to fear, anxiety, depression, and excuse making because we're unable to cope with the excess stress.

The ultimate paradox is that stress is the substance that can either bolster our physiological and psychological well-being or cripple it. The simple key to this paradox is knowing how to balance your stress so that it doesn't get out of control. Make no mistake about it; if you successfully balance your stress, you successfully balance your life.

Let's take a look inside your body so you can see just how this stress response works. If we understand this stress response, we can figure out how to balance it through exercise. Remember your nervous system is designed to avoid pain and seek pleasure. The brain is armed with a specific mechanism called the amygdala, which is responsible for taking in both the good and the bad emotions you experience.

> Make no mistake about it; if you successfully balance
> your stress, you successfully balance your life.

The amygdala in primal times first triggered the stress response (the fight-or-flight response) that allowed our ancestors to escape bears or saber-toothed tigers. When this center of the brain is triggered by a stressful event, it begins a hormonal cascade that flows through what scientists have called the HPA axis—the hypothalamus, pituitary, adrenal glands. The stress response always follows that order.

John J. Ratey, MD, gives an excellent description of this response in his book, *Spark:*

> Within ten milliseconds of sounding the alarm, the amygdala fires off messages that cause the adrenal gland to release different hormones at different stages. First, norepinephrine triggers lightning-fast electrical impulses that travel through the sympathetic nervous system activate the adrenal gland to dump the hormone epinephrine, or adrenaline, into the bloodstream. Heart rate, blood pressure, and breathing increase, contributing to the physical agitation that we feel under stress. At the same time, signals carried by norepinephrine to the corticotropin-releasing factor (CRF) travel from the amygdala to the hypothalamus, where they are handed off to messengers that take the slow train through the bloodstream. These messengers prompt the pituitary gland to activate another part of the adrenal gland, which releases the second major hormone of the stress response: cortisol. This relay from the hypothalamus to the pituitary to the adrenal gland is known as the HPA axis, and its role in summoning cortisol and in turning off the response makes it a key player in the story of stress.[13]

Our HPA axis is activated to generate stress hormones, such as adrenaline and cortisol, to give us the energy we need to flee from danger. In modern life we rarely encounter life-threatening circumstances, but our brains still release these powerful hormones to help us deal with the demands of everyday life. In our westernized lifestyle, we have largely equated success with how much money we make and what we have acquired materially. We've told ourselves that if we make a six-figure income and wear twenty different hats both professionally and personally, we are sophisticated.

This constant drive for success has created an overabundance of stress that ultimately leads to the overproduction of cortisol. The overabundance of

---

[13]   Ibid.

cortisol has a corrosive effect on the neurons in your brain. This can lead to the breakdown of your brain by eroding key neuronal connections responsible for long- and short-term memory. It can also put you into a state of chronic catabolism or physical breakdown. When this happens, your ability to think logically and to see the world as a loving and exciting place is compromised.

Cortisol also eats away at a part of your brain known as the hippocampus. Your hippocampus is largely in charge of putting your emotions into context. It does this by keeping another part of your brain, the amygdala, in check. Your amygdala takes in the *content* of your environment, whereas your hippocampus puts the content into proper *context*.

If the hippocampus is compromised by excessive cortisol, your amygdala can become hypersensitive to environmental stimuli and create inappropriate levels of fear, anxiety, and trepidation. That's because your hippocampus has been eroded by excessive cortisol and is not strong enough to translate the essentials of emotional context.

Exercise helps create a low level of stress in the brain and helps fortify it against higher levels of stress. It does this by stimulating the hormones and growth factors responsible for bolstering brain neurons. In other words, when you exercise, your ability to handle stress increases dramatically because it bolsters the physical components of the brain, such as the hippocampus, that are sensitive to the effects of excessive cortisol.

This is akin to building a house made of straw versus a house made of brick. When the tornado of life approaches, and your cortisol levels rise, your brain has the protection of stronger infrastructure so that cortisol can't penetrate it easily.

Observe this in your peers. Those who exercise regularly typically have a higher tolerance for stress and trauma. And your sedentary friends are often stressed and in a state of whining and complaining. The world never seems to be right with them, and there is good reason for this: their brain is slowly being eroded by cortisol. Of course, there are exceptions to this rule; typically people who exercise regularly have a positive disposition and outlook on life.

Let's summarize this in contemporary terms. When you get into a habit of negative thinking, eating poorly, and not exercising, you create a massive amount of stress in your body. This stress activates your sympathetic nervous system and dumps cortisol into your blood. Excessive cortisol slowly eats away at the key elements of your brain that help you use logic and have poise. Under these conditions, can you live an excuse-free life when your brain is literally being eaten alive.

The Nitty-Gritty of Your Neurotransmitters

Unless you still believe in Santa Claus, chances are you've heard of antidepressant drugs. The most popular class of these drugs is selective serotonin reuptake inhibitors (SSRIs). Serotonin is one of your brain's primary neurotransmitters and is partially responsible for maintaining calm and a sense of well-being. Other classes of antidepressant drugs work on other key neurotransmitters, such as norepinephrine and dopamine. The proper balance of these and other neurotransmitters are largely responsible for your perceptions and overall happiness.

The problem with most of these drugs is that they selectively alter one of your primary neurotransmitters while not affecting the others. This leads to further imbalance and can create a host of undesirable side effects. While there might be a place for these drugs, this typical allopathic approach fails many people year after year and creates a list of side effects ranging from dependency to suicidal thoughts. This is certainly not a recipe for exorcising your excuses!

What if I were to tell you that there's a natural way to balance your serotonin, norepinephrine, and dopamine? Would you do it? As you may have guessed by now, exercise is a powerful antidepressant and anti-anxiety agent. Numerous studies have compared the effects of exercise against antidepressant drugs, and in most cases, the exercise control groups found more relief than the group consuming antidepressant drugs. In all cases, exercise has no undesirable side effects and creates positive physiological effects, such as endorphin release.

Exercise affects our mood through the natural regulation of our primary neurotransmitters. Ratey states,

> Aside from elevating endorphins, exercise regulates all of the neurotransmitters targeted by antidepressants. For starters, exercise immediately elevates levels of Schildkraut's favorite neurotransmitter, norepinephrine, in certain areas of the brain. It wakes up the brain and gets it going and improves self-esteem, which is one component of depression.
>
> Exercise also boosts dopamine, which improves mood and feelings of wellness and jump-starts the attention system. Dopamine is all about motivation and attention. Studies have shown that chronic exercise increases dopamine storage in the brain and also triggers the production of enzymes that create dopamine receptors in the reward center of the brain, and this provides a feeling of satisfaction when we have accomplished something. If the demand is there, the dopamine genes get activated to produce more, and the overall effect is a more stable regulation of these pathways, which are important to controlling addictions.
>
> Serotonin is equally affected by exercise, and it's important for mood, impulse control, and self-esteem. It also helps stave off stress by counteracting cortisol, and it primes the cellular connections in the cortex and hippocampus that are important for learning.[14]

Ratey teaches us that exercise is highly effective at balancing the neurotransmitters that are largely responsible for our moods, perceptions, and well-being. Keep in mind that even the most powerful of drugs don't possess this ability.

---

[14] Ibid.

So, the next time you find yourself depressed or anxious, remember that you can short-circuit your lousy thoughts with exercise or brisk movement. The cool thing about body movement is that you can do it on the spot. If you're having a hard time maintaining a positive mind-set, you can exercise your way into a supercharged mind-set and ditch toxic thinking.

Try this out: The next time you find yourself having a negative internal dialogue or making excuses for no apparent reason, try exercising. Literally stop what you're doing, and put your body into motion. Whenever my mind turns south or I feel like excusing life away, I immediately jump rope or do a battle ropes workout for ten to fifteen minutes. This restarts my prefrontal cortex and balances my neurotransmitters. Without fail, I can always think and reason much more clearly, and to the delight of my peers, my mood receives an instant boost.

Here's an important point: we all have bad days and moments of toxic thinking. That is part of being a human being, and it's 100 percent acceptable. But *consciously remaining* in that state of mind isn't acceptable. When this happens to you, acknowledge your feelings, learn from them, and exercise the hell out of them. In the next chapter, I'll make simple suggestions for making exercise a regular part of your life.

If you neglect to move your body and your mind, you enable negative internal dialogues to stick around too long, which trains your brain to think in a negative pattern. This is called the law of facilitation, and it literally defines your world and your well-being. It's your turn to be proactive by being physically active. It's worth the very small price you pay.

Identify the Movement of Your Life

Now let's consider the movement of your life. Do you have a dream and an overarching goal? Have you crafted your Crystal-Clear Vision? Are you moving toward your dream or away from your dream? Remember— without a dream or a target, there can be no movement. And when you don't move, you invoke the negating forces of stagnancy, complacency, mediocrity, and apathy.

Frequently ask yourself, *Is my life moving in the direction that I desire?* If your answer is no, ask yourself why not. The answer should have nothing to do with your external circumstances. Even when life throws you the hardest of curve balls, you can still flow and move in the direction of your dream. I will often convince myself that I'm making all the right decisions yet nothing seems to go my way. In these moments I must ask, "What is my Highest Self trying to teach me now?"

> Without a dream or a target, there can be no movement.
> And when you don't move, you invoke the negating forces
> of stagnancy, complacency, mediocrity, and apathy.

It takes spiritual maturity to listen to your Highest Self and know that it won't lead you astray. Your soul will tell you if you're moving in the right direction, and it will warn you when you stray from your intended spiritual path. The key is to listen to your Highest Self and not allow the conditioned beliefs and expectations of your ego to contend with your inner compass. When you're wise enough to listen to your soul, it will take you on a journey that can be described only as a journey of faith. When you explore this journey, you'll find excitement and movement in your life that seems to whisper, "You're doing the right thing."

> When you're wise enough to listen to your soul, it will take you on
> a journey that can be described only as a journey of faith. When
> you explore this journey, you'll find excitement and movement in
> your life that seems to whisper, "You're doing the right thing."

You will sense the culmination of inner movement when you integrate the movement of your body, mind, emotions, and spirit. All these elements require movement, and movement is created by daily challenging yourself in all these areas.

In the following conclusion, you'll learn how to apply the concepts and principles that you've learned up to this point. It's time to meet and live from your Highest Self. It is truly time to exorcise your excuses.

CONCLUSION

EXERCISING AND YOUR EXCUSE EXORCISMS

Overthinking is often the product of underdoing.
—Yehuda Berg

Well, my friend, you made it! I'd like say you've reached the end of your journey, but I would be lying. In truth, you have just begun a lifelong journey. You have received a priceless gift: *awareness*. You have experienced this wonderful gift throughout this book, and you can continue to bring awareness into your life.

When we live unaware of our motivations, thinking patterns, and conditioned beliefs, we are vulnerable to the onslaught of excuse making. You now possess knowledge that is both liberating and mandating. It's liberating because you have all the tools necessary to rid yourself of negatively conditioned beliefs that lead to excuse making.

With newly acquired knowledge comes a mandate. You are accountable for putting this knowledge into action within your own life. In my opinion, there is nothing on God's green earth that can strip you of your character faster than having empty knowledge. When you're blessed with knowledge that allows you to act on your limitless potential, it's your responsibility to do so.

My overarching message is one of *love*. We all came from a place of unconditional love. We came from a place of creation, expression, expansion, and exploration. We came from the Source that doesn't and can't make excuses. Our Source is a source of love, compassion, and progression. If we accept this to be true, we must ask ourselves a very important follow-up question: "If I came from a source that is capable of achieving anything and doesn't have the capacity to make excuses, how can I make excuses?"

As human beings, we often define ourselves with labels. These labels tend to break us into tiny little pieces as they attempt to compartmentalize our very essence. You may be labeled as a professional, a parent, a lover, a brother, a sister, a failure, a warrior, or a student. Yet you can't be labeled accurately, because it's impossible to be compartmentalized, broken down, or separated from your true essence.

What is your true essence? It's the part of you that resonates with and is infinitely connected to your Creator, your Source. It makes no difference if you refer to this essence as God, Spirit, Consciousness, or Universe. It's imperative that you shed man-made labels and remember that you possess the same divine qualities as your Source.

Become one with the truth that you're created from a Source that's incapable of excuse making. You came from a Source that wants to experience life in the fullest. You came from a Source that doesn't say no. You came from a Source that says yes to life, to adventure, to health and fitness, and to exploration, happiness, fulfillment, and joy.

Here are my final questions: Will you settle for a life of mediocrity? Will you continue to entertain internal dialogues that cripple your character and your personal development? Will you continue to limit your own inner greatness by living by the dictates and expectations of another? Will you take this opportunity to better your life and become acquainted with your new self, the self that has been there all along, your Highest Self?

Your Highest Self is always in communion with your Source. In fact, it *is* your Source. It is now your privilege and your responsibility to live your life without the constraints of self-imposed boundaries created by excuse making.

Never excuse away your inner greatness, and always remember that life is good!

In addition to owning and operating Lifelong Fitness in Kaysville, Utah, Griff Neilson is also a well-known public speaker and entrepreneur with an avid passion for health and fitness. His many areas of specialization include the science of sugar addiction, holistic health and personal development. In addition to his professional research, Griff is also a multiple certified personal trainer and a Level III CHEK Holistic Lifestyle Coach. He graduated from the University of Utah in Exercise and Sports Science and has presented his FitMent Infinity and Sugar Freedom programs to multiple corporations, ranging from mid-sized businesses to Fortune 500 Companies.

Griff's books & programs are unique in that they blend personal development with personal health and fitness. Specifically, at the core of Griff's belief is the synergy between both the power of the mind, body and spirit in changing a person's lifestyle.

Printed in the United States
By Bookmasters